Publisher, Author and Creative Director
KARIE WESTERMANN

Photography and Artwork
DAVID FRASER

Technical Editor
AMELIA HODSDON, assisted by MICHELLE HAZELL

Copy Editor
KATE GREGORY

Book Design
JULES AKEL

Yarn Support
BLACKER YARNS, DYENINJA YARNS,
RIPPLES CRAFTS YARNS AND TRAVELKNITTER YARNS

Knitting Technicians
ELLY DOYLE, KATHERINE LYMER, LIZ MARLEY AND KARIE WESTERMANN

Shot on location at Innerpeffray Library, Perthshire, Scotland
with additional photography shot in Glasgow, Scotland

Printed and published in the U.K., 2017

British Library Cataloguing in Publication data
A catalogue record for this book is available from the British Library.

ISBN-978-1-5272-1315-9

THIS
THING
OF
PAPER

CONTENTS

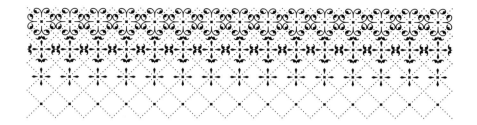

INTRODUCTION

Who is ignorant of the difference between writing [scriptura] and printing [impressura]?
A manuscript, written on parchment, can last a thousand years. How long will print,
this thing of paper [res papirea] last?

JOHANNES TRITHEMIUS
In Praise of Scribes (De Laude Scriptorum)

Book historians remember Johannes Trithemius for a late-fifteenth-century pamphlet in which he argues that the fragile, ugly products of the printing press will never match the durable, magnificent creations of the skilled scribe's pen.

While This Thing of Paper owes its title to a grumpy Benedictine abbot, the real spark of inspiration comes from Johannes Gutenberg and the invention of the printing press c.1450.

I have long been fascinated by how one invention could change the course of history and the printing press can definitely lay claim to doing just that. Before Gutenberg and his contemporaries, book production in Western Europe was a long and laborious process. Books were produced in small numbers by highly skilled craftsmen—typically monks—and these manuscripts were rare objects, reserved for a small elite of the clergy and nobility.

In many ways, the invention of the printing press brought about changes very similar to the changes brought about by the internet in today's world. The invention of movable type meant that books became more accessible and knowledge could spread much faster among a far greater number of people than previously. Rather than rely on ecclesiastical authority to decide what knowledge was precious enough to be immortalised in a manuscript, the printing press allowed people to preserve and discuss ideas that may not have always pleased those in power.

While writing this book, I have worked extensively with primary sources ranging from fourteenth-century illuminated manuscripts to sixteenth-century German embroidery manuals. I have also drawn upon my own background in book history as well as visiting historic sites in the U.K., Denmark, and Germany. The Gutenberg Museum in Mainz, Germany has been particularly helpful with my enquiries and I spent a very happy day working at the museum in December 2016, while the University of Glasgow's decision to put on an exhibition of early printed books at the Hunterian Museum in 2015 was extremely well-timed. Photographs were shot at Innerpeffray Library, Scotland's oldest lending library. I have drawn upon primary sources to define the colour palette and design vocabulary found throughout this book. It is important to note that I have not attempted to reconstruct any fourteenth-, fifteenth- or sixteenth-century garments—that has not been the aim of this book—but rather that I have let my research guide my design instincts.

Within this book you will find patterns inspired by vellum, the first printed books, mark making, illuminated capitals, quills scratching across the surface of a page, woodcuts, and the spines of books in a library. All the patterns in This Thing of Paper form parts of a book, both figuratively and literally. They are divided into three distinct stories.

Story 1: MANUSCRIPT. The story of handmade manuscripts and the people who worked on making them. Sources are mainly fourteenth-century manuscripts.

Story 2: INVENTION. The story of the period in which Johannes Gutenberg and his contemporaries transformed book production in Western Europe. Sources are early printed books produced between circa 1440 and 1501.

Story 3: PRINTED. The story of when printed matter became more commonplace and how people en-gaged with printed books. Sources

are mostly sixteenth and seventeenth century books.

As a knitter, I find the connections and parallels between knitting and books compelling. The move from something handmade to machine-made is one which is perhaps most poignant to us knitters as the world keeps reminding us it would be quicker (and probably cheaper) if we bought a machine-knitted garment rather than insisted on making it ourselves. And yet we persist. I have attempted to untangle some of these connections in the essays which accompany the patterns. Some essays are slightly academic in tone; others essays are more personal. I hope they give you pause for thought and make you contemplate your own relationships with making, consumption and communication. ☞

I.I

MANUSCRIPT

— · —

VELLUM

Prepared animal skin used as a writing surface and material.

— · —

We must expect great innovations to transform the entire technique of the arts, thereby affecting artistic invention itself and perhaps even bringing about an amazing change in our very notion of art.

PAUL VALÉRY
Pièces sur L'Art, 1931

❦

I often marvel at how we take a trip to the book-shop or the library for granted; how we think nothing of seeing books in people's houses; how charity shops sell books for a pittance, and how some restaurants use books as props rather than as objects to read.

I often marvel at how we can walk into a clothes shop and pay £7 for a brand-new cardigan or spend a pound in a charity shop on the same cardigan six months later; how fast fashion moves, with clothes no longer expected to last more than a season; how casually clothes are being described (is this wool? Acrylic? Knit or crochet?).

Books are an interior design feature; clothes are something you discard after a few wears.

Somehow we have ended up in a world where consumption makes you and you don't make what you consume. The last thirty years have also seen a massive change in how we communicate, how we live, and how we relate to the things we own. As we live our lives via screens — whether reading books we downloaded from online retailers just seconds earlier or documenting our #ootd (outfit of the day) — I'm struck by how we seem to engage with physical things in an indirect way. Items that end up in our hands or on our bodies seem increasingly ephemeral. Paradoxically, the more materialistic we become, the more immaterial the material things in our lives seem.

Books are no longer rare items; clothes are not something you mend and care for.

How can we place a value on an item when we cannot relate to its material qualities? How can we avoid seeing an item as disposable when we have easy access to many more (seemingly identical) items?

These questions are not new. We have been asking them since the first mass-produced items began appearing. Modernity carries anxiety in its hands.

The idea of 'presence' is central here. We talk about people having 'presence'—a certain sense of charisma, perhaps—but 'presence' can also be extended to items. A painting seems somehow more substantial than a photo, and a card is more personal than a text message. Why do paintings feel more important? Why are cards more special than text messages?

One answer would be that they are the products of specific human hands. We know that a painting by Paul Gauguin will have been made by the artist himself—his hands will have transferred a sense of his 'being-there' (or his 'being-in-time') to his work. A reproduction of a Gauguin painting will not carry the same sense of 'being-there'—the artist will be at a remove.

Another answer is an extension

of that. Think of a medieval manuscript. We may not know the specific scribe who produced the object, but we know that someone (or several someones) were there to make it. Making a manuscript involved multiple processes and many specialist people. You had to raise animals (primarily calves and sheep) for the vellum, and prepare the hides; you had to produce ink from bark or soot (one recipe I found contained seven separate stages to turn one hawthorn branch into ink — and involved a lot of wine!); you had to make writing tools by curing goose feathers; if you wanted illuminations, you had to make your own paints which would involve growing plants or sourcing minerals from as far away as Afghanistan — and you would also need small amounts of precious metals. Again, a reproduction will not have the same sense of catching a glimpse of other human beings.

The Vellum cardigan pays tribute to the beautiful materials used in making books at the time. It also explores some of the colours often found in manuscripts. I wanted to think about the yarn travelling through my hands and think about the process of making something I was going to wear. I thought about the process of making the yarn and chose to use materials where I knew the provenance. I know the hands that worked on making the yarn and the places in which it was created. And I knew I would not be able to make the cardigan overnight.

I wanted to explore the sense of presence in the Vellum cardigan — and I have purposefully avoided imitating or reproducing specific manuscripts. Instead I sought to explore the idea of inserting ourselves into the process of making. While you will technically be making the cardigan from my instructions, you will be knitting the piece itself with your own hands using yarn you have chosen yourself. Your Vellum will not be a mass-produced item, but something that will carry the trace of your own 'being-in-time'. ☞

VELLUM CARDIGAN

Materials

Blacker Yarns Tamar Lustre Blend DK (DK; 220m/241 yds per 100g ball/skein; 100% wool)

4 (4, 4, 5, 5, 6, 7) skeins in Ottery (A)

1 skein in Tresillian (B)

1 (1, 1, 1, 1, 1, 2) skeins in Red River (C)

1 skein in Camel (D)

Needles Used

3.25mm/US 3 DPNs or preferred needles for small circumferences

3.25m/US 3, circular, 80cm/32" or length comfortable for circumference

4mm/US 6, DPNs or preferred needles for small circumferences

4mm/US 6, circular, 80cm/32" or length comfortable for circumference

Gauge

20 sts x 28 rows = 10cm x 10cm/4" x 4" measured over st st on larger needles

Accessories

Waste yarn

7 (7, 7, 8, 8, 8, 8) buttons 20mm/.78"

Sizing

XS (S, M, L, 1X, 2X, 3X) to fit 68 (78, 88, 98, 108, 118, 128) cm/ 26.75 (30.75, 34.5, 38.5, 42.5, 46.5, 50.25)" bust with 5cm/2" ease. Please see schematic for details.

Pattern Notes

This pattern is suitable for intermediate knitters.

The cardigan is yoked, worked bottom-up in the round with a front steek.

TIP: if you find Sleeve Chart Rnds 5-11 to have a slightly looser tension than your colourwork rnds, try going down a needle size on these rnds (eg. to a 3.75mm/US 5).

For the body section, front steek sts are the first and last 3 sts of each round.

For the yoke section, front steek sts are the first 3 sts of each rnd followed by the Yoke chart being worked 28 (31, 33, 36, 38, 40, 43) times across the sts, then 1 st is worked to ensure the yoke pattern is centered at the front before 3 steek sts are worked as previously established.

INSTRUCTIONS

Body

Using col A and smaller circular needles, cast on 143 (167, 183, 207, 223, 247, 263) sts. Join to work in the rnd, being careful not to twist. Pm to mark beg of rnd.

Rnd 1: k3, *k1, p1; rep from * to last 4 sts, k4.

Rep Rnd 1 another 19 times.

Change to larger needles.

Work in st st for 19 (19, 21, 21, 23, 23, 23) rnds.

Next Rnd: k37 (43, 47, 53, 57, 63, 67), pm, k68 (80, 88, 100, 108, 120, 128), pm, k38 (44, 48, 54, 58, 64, 68).

Waist Shaping

Waist Shaping Rnd 1 (dec): *k to 3 sts before marker, ssk, k1, sm, k1, k2tog; rep from * once more, k to end. 139 (163, 179, 203, 219, 243, 259) sts

Waist Shaping Rnd 2: knit.

Work Waist Shaping Rnds 1 and 2 once more. 135 (159, 175, 199, 215, 239, 255) sts

Work in st st for 10 rnds.

Waist Shaping Rnd 3 (inc): *k to 3 sts before marker, m1, k1, sm, k1, m1; rep from * once more, k to end. 139 (163, 179, 203, 219, 243, 259) sts

Waist Shaping Rnd 4: knit.

Work Waist Shaping Rnds 3 and 4 once more. 143 (167, 183, 207, 223, 247, 263) sts

Work in st st for 42 (42, 42, 44, 44, 46, 46) rnds.

Next Rnd: *k to 2 (2, 2, 4, 4, 4, 4) sts before marker, cast off next 4 (4, 4, 8, 8, 8, 8) removing side markers in the process, rep from * once more, and k to end of round.

135 (159, 175, 191, 207, 231, 247) sts

Put body on waste yarn
or spare needles.

Sleeves

Using col A and smaller needles, cast
on 40 (40, 40, 48, 48, 48, 56) sts. Join
to work in the rnd, being careful not
to twist. Pm to mark beg of rnd.

Rnd 1: *k1, p1; rep from * to end.

Rep Rnd 1 another 9 times.

Change to larger needles. Work
Sleeve chart over the next 22 rnds.
42 (42, 42, 50, 50, 50, 58) sts

Continue to work st st in col A.

Work all sleeve increases as
foll: k1, m1, k to last st from
end, m1, k1. 2 sts increased.

Work increase rnd every 10th
(10th, 10th, 6th, 6th, 4th, 4th)
rnd, 3 (3, 3, 0, 2, 10, 5) times. 48
(48, 48, 50, 54, 70, 68) sts

Work increase rnd every 14th
(14th, 14th, 12th, 8th, 8th, 6th)
rnd, 4 (4, 4, 7, 9, 5, 10) times. 56
(56, 56, 64, 72, 80, 88) sts.

Next Rnd: remove marker, cast
off 2 (2, 2, 4, 4, 4, 4) sts, k to last
2 (2, 2, 4, 4, 4, 4) sts, cast off rem
sts. 52 (52, 52, 56, 64, 72, 80) sts

Place rem sts on waste
yarn or spare needles.

Work second sleeve the same.

Joining Body for the Yoke

Now join sts to work yoke as
outlined below by knitting across
sts in the following sequence:
left front, pm, sleeve, pm, back,
pm, sleeve, pm, right front. 247
(271, 287, 319, 351, 391, 423) sts

Yoke Shaping Rnd 1: *k to 3 sts bef
marker, k2tog, k1, sm, k1, ssk; rep
from * another 3 times, k to end.

Yoke Shaping Rnd 2: knit. 239
(263, 279, 311, 343, 383, 415) sts

Work Yoke Shaping Rnds 1 and
2 another 1 (1, 1, 2, 4, 7, 8) times.
231 (255, 271, 295, 311, 327, 351) sts

Work 3 (8, 11, 12, 11,
7, 8) rnds in st st.

Over the next 44 rnds, work Steek
and Yoke charts across the rnd.

Work Steek chart, work Yoke
chart 28 (31, 33, 36, 38, 40, 43)
times, work Steek chart. 91 (100,
106, 115, 121, 127, 136) sts

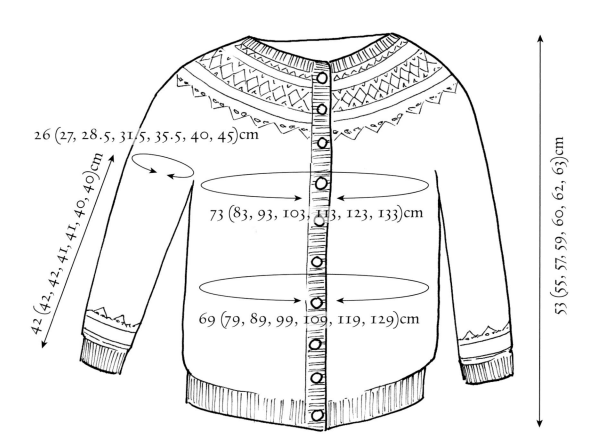

26 (27, 28.5, 31.5, 35.5, 40, 45)cm

42 (42, 42, 41, 41, 40, 40)cm

73 (83, 93, 103, 113, 123, 133)cm

69 (79, 89, 99, 109, 119, 129)cm

53 (55, 57, 59, 60, 62, 63)cm

Sizes

Sizes S and M:

Next Rnd: k46 (49) sts, k2tog, k to end. 99 (105) sts

Size 2X:

Next Rnd: k31, k2tog, k62, k2tog, k to end. 125 sts

Size 3X:

Next Rnd: k3, *k9, k2tog; rep from to last 12 sts, k12. 125 sts

All sizes:

Begin neckline.

Rnd 1: k3, *k1, p1; rep from * to last 4 sts, k4.

Rep Rnd 1 another 7 times. Cast off.

Steek

Following instructions on steeking (see Special Techniques, page 129), cut the front steek sts. Gently use steam to allow the fabric to relax before working on the buttonband.

Buttonband

Right buttonband:

With RS facing, start at the bottom right edge and, using smaller circular needles, pick up and k105 (107, 111, 115, 117, 121, 123) sts.

Row 1 (WS): p1, *k1, p1; rep from * to last st.

Rows 2-3: work in rib patt as est.

Row 4 (RS): work in patt for 3 (4, 3, 4, 5, 3, 4) sts, then *work buttonhole, patt for 12 (12, 13, 11, 11, 12, 12) sts; rep from * another 5 (5, 5, 6, 6, 6, 6) times, work buttonhole, work 2 (3, 2, 2, 3, 2, 3) sts in pattern;

Rows 5-9: work in rib patt as est.

Cast off in patt.

Left buttonband:

With RS facing, start at the top left edge and, using smaller circular needles, pick up and k105 (107, 111, 115, 117, 121, 123) sts.

Row 1 (WS): p1, *k1, p1; rep from * to end.

Rows 2-9: work in rib patt as est.

Cast off in patt.

Noting placement of buttonholes, sew on buttons. Weave in ends.

Yoke   Sleeve   Steek   Key

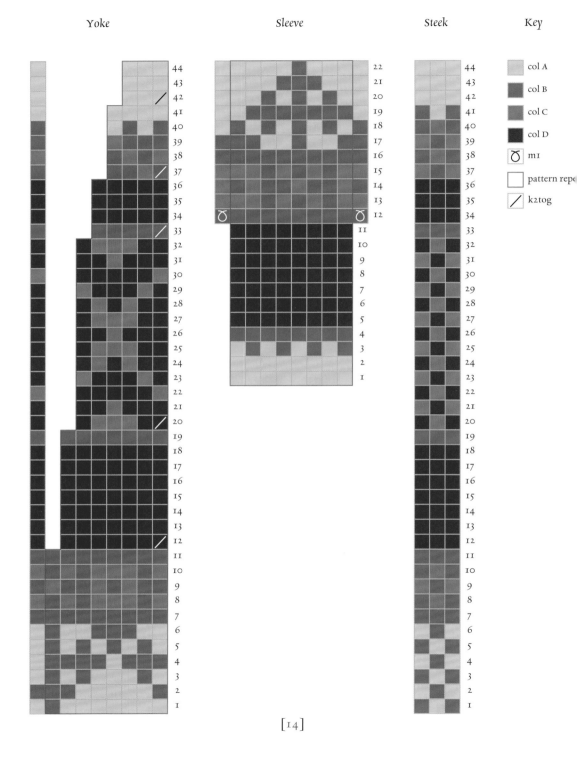

I.2

MANUSCRIPT

———— • ————

SCRIPTORIUM

A room in medieval monasteries where scribes copied, illuminated
and wrote down manuscripts.

———— • ————

*One word cannot be lost [from a poem] but the whole work fails…Every word having his
natural seat, which seat must needs make the words remembered.*

SIR PHILIP SIDNEY
Apology for Poesy, 1580

am fascinated by how our hands and bodies influence our making.

Remember being a child trying to write neatly? My teacher would look over my shoulder as my letters changed from unsure scribbles that looked like As (or Gs or Os depending upon the time of day and my level of concentration) to confidently joined-up letters. Now my Gs always look neat, my Fs flirt with being flamboyant, while my Ss look hurried. And I can tell by my handwriting if I have written something while being tired or when distracted—the difference is particularly noticeable in how the Ms and Ns are joined.

Knitting contains similar stories.

Remember your first hesitant stitches and the uneven edge stitches that somehow kept multiplying? The time it took to finish a row, only to realise you had dropped a stitch on the row below? Then your hands became more confident: your tension evened out and you no longer twisted stitches without realising it? And, finally, your hands became expert and you no longer have to watch the stitches as you made them. Your hands have acquired knowledge and suddenly the stitches flow across the needles, much like those joined-up Ms and Ns. Working k1, p1 feels almost effortless.

Writing and knitting are not that different. We use the same tools and materials—pen and needles; ink, paper and yarn—and we perform the same motions with our hands, carefully forming letters or purls. Ideas in our heads become material reality through the careful movements of our hands. Emotions expressed through motion. Yet the outcome of our work varies from person to person. The end result is the same item whether it be a scarf or a postcard, but how we get there and how the result looks is always highly individual. Your handwriting might be angular or rounded or cursive; you might be a tight or a loose knitter or your purl stitches might be slightly looser than your knit stitches.

Our hands contain knowledge and create meaning.

I came back to knitting at a time when I was very ill. I could not read my beloved books, nor could I watch TV or listen to the radio. My brain was incapable of capturing meaning beyond a few minutes, rendering most plots incomprehensible to me. I was in bed for several months and could do nothing to mark the passage of time. Somehow I came upon the idea of knitting a scarf. It seemed an attainable task from my position in bed. As a child I had been a competent, but essentially apathetic, knitter making things for my dolls. Later I had knitted most of a cardigan for a friend expecting a baby (my mother knitted the sleeves—even then I struggled with sleeves!). Surely I would be able to manage a few stitches every day? My partner bought me yarn and needles and I asked him to bring me the laptop so I could look up instructions on how to cast on. 'Look at your hands', he countered. I looked down. My hands were casting on stitches while my brain was frantically trying to remember how to get started. When I could not trust my brain to retain a plot or pay attention for more than a few minutes, my hands' memories of carefully forming stitches were still inside my body.

My grandmother had a stroke not long after I began writing this book. She has become an unreliable narrator of her own life as years are wiped away and relationships forgotten. Forty years of accumulated wisdom and regrets, lost in a day. I visited her in hospital—once a hale woman of farm stock, now a frail little lady in a hospital gown. She did not remember her own brother; but when a nurse gave her a set of needles, my grandmother started knitting.

We write stories with our stitches; stitches are tiny letters combined to tell a tale.

Knitters have an impulse to create, a desire to 'make stuff'. We have a spark inside of us that wants out; to be released through our hands manipulating materials. We have a desire to write our own stories through the yarn we choose, the places we knit, and the item we have decided to make. The grand stories are writ materially through the making of wedding shawls or baby blankets. Smaller, more intimate stories are told in other items: the hat you knitted in the rose garden, the socks you knitted during your lunch breaks in your old job, and the scarf you knitted furiously on that disastrous cruise you took with Aunt Jennifer.

Poiesis is an ancient Greek term that philosophers use when discussing how humans take an idea and make it into reality. The notion that we can retain knowledge in our minds and bodies (such as how to cast on) and turn that knowledge into an object through creativity is one that is arguably uniquely human. The Greek philosopher Aristotle distinguished between knowledge (*episteme*), craft (*techne*), process (*praxis*) and bringing-forth (*poiesis*). The first three terms are relatively easy to understand: the knowledge needed to make something, the method or craft used in making and the process of making something — but where does that leave *poiesis*? It is the divine little spark that creates the idea in the first place; the impulse to make; the desire to bring into being something that did not exist before: it is creation. *Poiesis* articulates that knowledge which is in our heads, the knowledge that wants out through our practised hands and into the world through our chosen craft: the truth that is personally ours.

Knitting is a craft and a process brought about by our knowledge — a knowledge that is embedded in both our brains and our bodies. But I would argue that knitting is very much *poiesis* as well.

The word 'poetry' is derived from poiesis — its deep meaning left behind in the Scots word for poet, *makar*. Poets are makers; makers are poets. Poetry is language that crafts meaning through layered repetition. Nowadays poetry may be regarded as

difficult and niche, but it makes up much of our oldest surviving literature. Before the advent of writing (let alone printing!), repetition made sure that stories were handed down from generation to generation. Something in our brains is hardwired to remember repeated sounds and beats (what we also know as rhyme and metre). It is this twin emphasis upon making and repetition that makes me think of knitting.

Knitting works on the basis of repetition too. Think of stitches such as simple knits and purls. Now, read the following: *k1, p1; rep from* to end. Those singular knits and purls once repeated create a row of ribbing. And if that row of ribbing is stacked directly on top of the previous row, we have a stable ribbed edging. If we move the stitch combination one stitch to the right, we create a different stitch pattern. Repetition creates pattern creates meaning. If stitches are letters and rows are lines, then a textile is a text with repetition creating structure and meaning.

The sound of a nib scratching the paper or the needles clacking. Words

on a page or stitches in a scarf. We craft sonnets and compose cardigans with our hands. We write our own lives into our making. ☞

SCRIPTORIUM MITTENS

Materials

Blacker Yarns Swan 4ply
(4ply; 175m/190 yds per
50 g ball; 100% wool)

1 ball each in Mountain Berry
(A), Hawkweed (B), Pale Maiden
(C) and Sky Grey (D)

XS/S sample used 90m/98 yds in col
A, 30m/32 yds in col B, 140m/153 yds
in col C, and 130m/142yds in col D.

Needles Used

For XS/S:

2.75mm/US 2 DPNs or preferred
needles for small circumferences

For M:

3.00mm/US 3 DPNs or preferred
needles for small circumferences

For L/XL:

3.25mm/US 3 DPNs or preferred
needles for small circumferences

Gauge

34 (32, 30) sts x 38 (36, 34) rows =
10cm x 10cm / 4" x 4" measured
over colourwork on needles
required for matching gauge

Accessories

Stitch marker

Waste yarn

Sizing

XS/S, M and L/XL to fit 18 (20,
21.5)cm / 7 (7.75, 8.5)" hand
circumference and 24 (26, 27.5)
cm / 9.5 (10 10.5)" total length

Pattern Notes

This pattern is suitable for

intermediate knitters.

The mittens are worked in the round using stranded knitting.

Catching long floats is recommended.

The mittens can be made longer or shorter by adding rounds of plan knitting after Rnd 2 of chart or by removing Rnds 1 and 2.

The thumb can be made longer by adding rounds of plain knitting before the decreases at the top.

INSTRUCTIONS

Both Hands

Using col A, cast on 64 sts and distribute sts evenly across needles.

Join to work in the rnd, being careful not to twist. Pm to mark beg of rnd.

Rnd 1: *k1, p1; rep from * to end.

Rnd 1 another 14 times.

Knit one rnd.

Work from chart for appropriate mitten, reading from right to left. Work front and then back, until you have reached the highlighted sts in Rnd 37. These sts indicate the thumb placement and differ

for left and right mittens. Make sure you work the correct one.

Next, using waste yarn, knit the next 10 sts, then break the yarn leaving a tail. Slide the just-knitted sts back on to LH needle. Now use the working yarn to continue in patt as indicated by the chart.

Continue to work in patt until Rnd 77 is completed. 10 sts

Work a three-needle cast-off on the rem sts as specified in Special Techniques, page 130.

Thumb

Carefully remove the waste yarn and, using col A, pick up and k 10 sts below the gap, 2 sts at the edge, 10 sts above the gap, and 2 sts at the other edge. 24 sts

Rnd 1: knit.

Work Rnd 1 another 19 times (or until thumb is desired length).

Rnd 1: [ssk, k8, k2tog] twice. 20 sts

Rnd 2: [ssk, k6, k2tog] twice. 16 sts

Rnd 3: [ssk, k4, k2tog] twice. 12 sts

Rnd 4: [ssk, k2, k2tog] twice. 8 sts

Break yarn, leaving a long tail. Draw

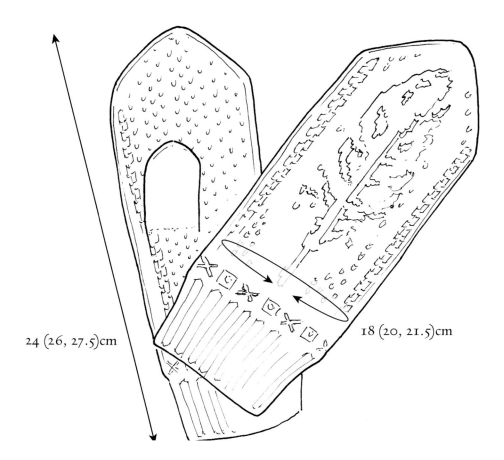

24 (26, 27.5)cm

18 (20, 21.5)cm

yarn through rem ſts and pull tight.

Make two, making sure to knit both a right hand and a left hand (take care with thumb placement).

Finishing

Weave in ends, but do not trim.

Use lengths of yarn to close any gaps surrounding the thumb gusset area.

Steam block gently to even out colourwork.

Once dry, trim ends.

Key

- col A
- col B
- col C
- col D
- Left Thumb
- Right Thumb
- k2tog
- ssk

Right

Left

Key

- col A
- col B
- col C
- col D
- Left Thumb
- Right Thumb
- k2tog
- ssk

Back

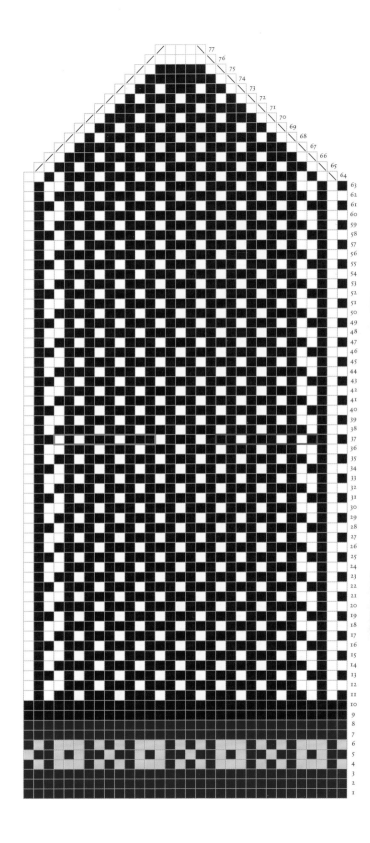

I.3

MANUSCRIPT

PSALTER

A book containing the Book of Psalms—
one of the most widely owned books of the medieval era.

Invited to a barbecue / I found refuge in the kitchen
Discussing post-war US literature / With a girl whose upper arm read fiction
Like it might have been typewritten.
I asked her its significance / She said she sometimes took reminding
What she wanted to be doing / Whether reading it or writing.

THE LUCKSMITHS
Fiction, 2005

❧

Books are dangerous. They make us imagine worlds beyond our own mundane experiences. They make us see the world as others see it. Books carry hope and promise.

During the early Middle Ages, most books were used for religious purposes by monks and priests. They were liturgical texts commissioned for monasteries and carefully illuminated to be symbols of the glory of God. The word 'illumination' was derived from the Latin *illuminare* (to 'be lit up') and refers to the reflected light coming from the gold leaves. The very format of the manuscripts was emblematic of the power of the words they contained. In the beginning was the Word, and the Word was with God, and the Word was God.

By the early twelfth century, books were becoming more secular. Reflecting a changing society, manuscripts began to be produced for individuals as well as the religious institutions. The earliest universities were founded, populations expanded, many new towns were built across Europe and the merchant class began coming into its own. The demand for books was higher than ever—both as status symbols and also for the knowledge they contained. Scribes were no longer confined to monasteries.

The Psalter shawl is an illuminated letter, a stylised blue C drawn on a background of beige vellum. The slip-stitch pattern is a nod to the geometric patterns found in many medieval manuscripts and also alludes to the tiled patterns crusaders and pilgrims would have seen on their travels. However, the Psalter shawl is named after one particular psalter, the Luttrell Psalter (now in the British Museum, London).

The Luttrell Psalter was commissioned in the mid-fourteenth century by Sir Geoffrey Luttrell, a landowner from Lincolnshire. He is depicted in a miniature portrait towards the end of the manuscript as a knight on horseback, fully armed and dazzling in his resplendent coat of arms. His wife and daughter-in-law are shown admiring him, dressed in gowns that complement Sir Geoffrey. His is not a subtle portrait—it positively reeks of importance and power.

However, the Luttrell Psalter is more than overt depictions of power and devotional depictions of saints and beasts. It is famous for showing detailed depictions of everyday life in the medieval world, something so rare to find. You see a women with a spindle feeding chickens; farmers tilling a field; peasants sowing seeds in spring (complete with a cheeky bird eating from the bag of seeds); men and women harvesting and hay-gathering. I particularly like the drawing of a small dog chasing birds! Not much art survives seven centuries, let alone art focused on everyday life and ordinary people.

The lovely drawings of the Luttrell Psalter belie what the manuscript actually does, though. It upholds the natural order of things, as understood by medieval society. Contorted monsters lurk on the pages reminding people of the many dangers that await if you step out of line. The world is safe and good as long as you keep within the realm and your known world, but things get topsy-turvy if you begin to question authority and power (the Psalter uses the amusing, yet potent, image of a monkey driving a cart to illustrate this). Have faith in your master who is good and wise and keeps chaos away—the master being Sir Geoffrey, of course. The placement of his portrait right across from an illuminated letter showing a king is no accident.

I like books like this—books that tell me about the society in which they were made and that also make me think about the world in which I am now reading them.

As a woman I am keenly aware of being told to 'know my place'. I am also very familiar with all the awful things that will happen to me if I step out of line: if I don't watch how I dress, I will encourage cruel monsters (and I will be the one to blame), and if I voice an opinion that challenges stratified society, my rights will be in question. I am allowed to exist and live my very ordinary life as long as I don't push against any boundaries.

Books are dangerous. Sir Geoffrey may have sought to use his Psalter to consolidate his position and emphasise the power he wielded, yet books have the ability to transport us and let us become part of something bigger than ourselves. The Luttrell Psalter makes me think of all the limitations others want to put upon us and how important it is that we never let ourselves be governed by fear.

We should continue to turn pages and wrap giant illuminated letters around our bodies, because we are the authors of our own books. ☞

PSALTER SHAWL

Materials

DyeNinja Camel Silk Fingering
(4ply; 400m/435yds per 100g
skein; 50% baby camel/50% silk)

1 skein in Dromedary (A)

2 skeins in Byzantium (B)

Needles Used

3.75mm/US 5, circular, 80cm/32"

Gauge

16 sts x 30 rows = 10cm x 10cm
/ 4" x 4" measured over st st

22 sts x 31 rows = 10cm x 10cm / 4"x
4" measured over slip-stitch pattern

Sizing

One size: 175cm x 70cm
/ 68.5" x 26.75"

Pattern Notes

This pattern is suitable for
intermediate knitters.

The shawl is worked top-down
and it uses slip-stitch techniques
and an applied edge.

Row gauge is more important
than stitch gauge as it determines
the size of the shawl. If your row
gauge is very different to the one
specified in the pattern, you may
wish to go up or down a needle
size. If you do so, please consider
the drape of your fabric.

Slip all stitches purlwise unless
specifically instructed otherwise.

An applied border is worked at a
90-degree angle to the shawl body
at the end. You cast on stitches, and
work them according to the chart. As
you reach the end of the border chart,
you join the last stitch of your border
to a stitch from the shawl body.

INSTRUCTIONS

Body

Using col A, cast on 8 sts.

Set-up Row (WS): k2, p4, k2.

Row 1 (RS, inc): k2, *m1, k1; rep from * to last 2 sts, m1, k2. 13 sts

Row 2 and all even rows: k2, p to last 2 sts, k2.

Row 3: knit.

Row 5 (inc): k2, *m1, k1; rep to last 2 sts, k2. 22 sts

Rows 7, 9 and 11: knit.

Row 13 (inc): k2, *m1, k1; rep to last 2 sts, k2. 40 sts

Rows 14-24: work even, maintaining edging.

Row 25 (inc): k2, *m1, k1; rep from * to last 2 sts, k2. 76 sts

Rows 26-50: work even, maintaining edging.

Row 51 (inc): k2, *m1, k1; rep from * to last 2 sts, k2. 148 sts

Rows 52-96: work even, maintaining edging.

Break col A, leaving a tail long enough to weave in later. Change to col B.

Rows 97 and 98: knit.

Row 99 (inc): k2, m1, kfb,

*m1, k1; rep from * to last 3 sts, m1, kfb, m1, k2. 295 sts

Row 100: knit.

Without breaking col B, rejoin col A.

Slip-Stitch Section

Rows 101-157: k2, work Chart A, k2. (Seven full repeats of chart.)

Break col A, leaving a tail long enough to weave in later. Continue in col B.

Rows 158-160: knit.

Applied Border

With WS facing, and using the knitted cast-on method, cast on 31 sts. Do not turn.

Set-up Row (WS): k30, k2tog with first st from shawl body. Turn.

Next Row (RS): knit. Turn.

Next Row (WS): k30, k2tog with first st from shawl body. Turn.

Work Chart B 73 times across shawl body sts. After working the final row, 1 shawl body st and 31 border sts rem.

Next Row (RS): knit. Turn.

Next Row (WS): k to last st from end, k2tog with first st from shawl body. Turn.

Cast off rem sts as foll: k2, *put
both sts back onto LH needle, k2tog
tbl, k1; rep from * until end.

Finishing

Weave in ends and block to
dimensions given in schematic.

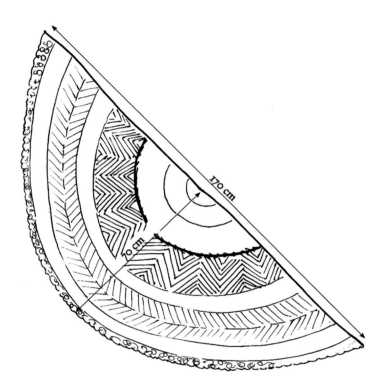

Key

◯	yo		col A	
╱	RS: ssk		col B	
╲	RS: k2tog / WS: p2tog		RS: knit / WS: purl	
◗	cast off	•	RS: purl / WS: knit	
▢	pattern repeat	⋁	RS: slip pwise wyib / WS: slip pwise wyif	

Chart A

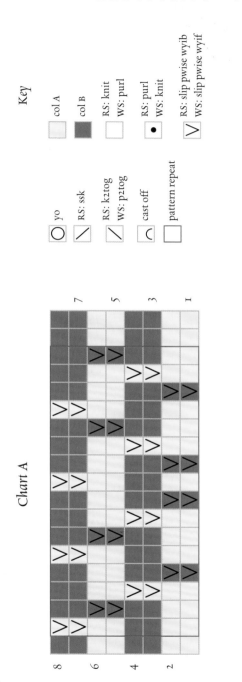

Chart B

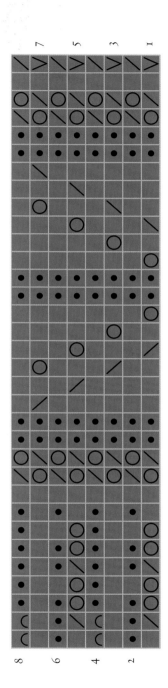

2.1

INVENTION

— • —

INCUNABULA

Books or pamphlets printed before 1501.

— • —

Print was busy with what print does.

ALLEN CURNOW
Lone Kauri Road, 1972

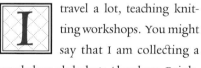I travel a lot, teaching knitting workshops. You might say that I am collecting a workshop alphabet: Aberdeen, Brighton, Copenhagen, Dundee...

Everywhere I go, I meet fantastic, brilliant knitters keen to show me what they have been making.

In Northern Ireland one time, I met Bee, a petite grey-haired lady in her 60s with a spark of anarchy in her eyes. I knew she would be trouble of the best kind. Bee had knitted herself a fantastic cabled coat out of red yarn. During the lunch break she twirled in front of me showing off the red coat and throwing shapes as though at a rock concert. I complimented Bee and told her that I loved both the coat and her attitude.

Then Bee began to point out all the places where she had made mistakes. I had not noticed that one uncrossed cable at the lower back; quite frankly, it was practically invisible unless you sat down on the floor, made Bee stop twirling for a minute, and looked at the hem very, very closely.

I was quite sad that this brilliant, vibrant woman felt the need to point out the mistakes in her red coat rather than embrace the fact that she had knitted a complex, beautiful garment.

I am going to tell you a story about imperfections.

In the mid-fifteenth century, a goldsmith called Johann Gutenberg invented a mechanical way of producing books. He had realised that book production would be both faster and easier if the individual letters of the alphabet were cut in reusable form. Using his knowledge as a goldsmith, he developed a way of producing small, identical letters that could be arranged to form any word. Around 1455, his experiments paid off and he produced the 42-line Bible, the first book made using movable type.

A few years ago I had the opportunity to try using a replica fifteenth-century printing press that had originally been built for a Stephen Fry programme on the BBC. I was surprised by several things. I knew that the first printing presses had been made from modified wine presses, but I was still taken aback at the size of the press and how many parts went into making it work.

Mostly, I was struck by how laborious the process was. While quicker than copying out an entire book by hand, it was still quite slow and very dependent upon labourers' hands. I smeared ink across the ink ball (pleasingly made from sheepskin and filled with wool), inked the type carefully, aligned the sheet of paper meticulously and pinned it down. Then I laid another sheet on top, folded over the frame, rolled this 'sandwich' under the press itself (called the platen), turned the handle so the platen would apply pressure, then turned the handle again so I could roll my 'sandwich' away again. I only printed one sheet and did not even have to typeset the page or make the ink, yet the process was absolutely exhausting and time-consuming. It was not until the late eighteenth century that printing became fully mechanised and streamlined. This fact blew my mind as I contemplated how many hands were involved in making a book. I kept looking at other participants' hands as they went through the many steps themselves.

Here is the important thing.

My printed sheet looked a bit wonky. The ink had not been distributed quite evenly and some of the text was a bit hard to read. In fact, every sheet being made that afternoon looked slightly different depending upon how well the ink had been applied or transferred. Even though we had all performed the same processes with the same tools, the sheets were all unique.

As part of my work on this book, I visited the Gutenberg Museum in Mainz, Germany (Gutenberg's home city). On the first floor, the museum holds two incomplete copies of Gutenberg's 42-line Bible, which I was allowed to examine under close

supervision. They were not identical. Quite apart from the differences owing to the printing process, they were also hand-finished by different rubricators and illuminators (as was the custom at the time). I was face-to-page with some of the most famous and most celebrated books in the world, and they looked a bit wonky too.

And so I think about all knitters who worry about their mistakes and their imperfections in their finished creations. Bee, who twirled with joy but stopped to tell me about that uncrossed cable. Susan, who forgot a yarnover early on and never finished her shawl as a result. Karen, who threw her knitting project into an open fire because she could not unsee her mistakes.

Why do we strive for perfection with such fervour? Why are we so hard on ourselves? Bee's red coat was truly beautiful, Susan's shawl was near completion, and nobody ever saw Karen's hard work before it met a fiery demise.

Imperfect handmade things can be far more meaningful and important than the perfection we seek. The uneven transfer of ink or a missed yarnover should not stop us from creating things. I tell people in my workshops to accept compliments, celebrate their beautiful work, and stop pointing out their mistakes. Non-knitters will not care about a missing yarnover or an uncrossed cable; knitters will understand.

But I should listen to myself.

One of the hardest parts of creating *This Thing of Paper* was that I was reading book upon book written by Very Important Men In Suits and all their books were Very Important Books With Footnotes. I found myself writing up against this pantheon of intimidation.

I had come to the library party carrying yarn in my hands and I felt all the words unravelling around my feet. The memories of working in book history all those years ago came rushing back and overwhelmed me. Bee's uncrossed cable became my hunting down a German philosopher; Susan's missing yarnover became three thousand words on the primacy of the written word. The small details tripped me up and made me lose sight of the whole — the beautiful thing I was creating. This project began with me feeling confident and happy because I knew about books. But to find my voice, I had to untangle myself from the years of being told to imitate the voices of Very Important Men In Suits, and that took a long time.

Finally, I am choosing to embrace the imperfections, the slight wonkiness and the fact that I am no longer writing for Very Important Men In Suits. I am going to write and knit and twirl. ☞

INCUNABULA CARDIGAN

Materials

Blacker Yarns British Classic DK (DK; 110m/119yds per 50g ball; 100% wool)

7 (7, 8, 9, 10, 11, 12) balls

Sample shown in Mustard

Needles Used

4mm/US 6, circular, 80cm/32" or length comfortable for circumference

4mm/US 6, DPNs or preferred needles for small circumferences

3.25mm/US 3, circular, 80cm/32" or length comfortable for circumference

3.25mm/US 3, DPNs or preferred needles for small circumferences

Gauge

20 sts x 24 rows = 10cm x 10cm / 4" x 4" measured over st pattern on larger needles

Accessories

7 (7, 8, 8, 9, 9, 9) buttons 17mm/.75"

7 stitch markers, two in each of cols A, B, C and one in col D

Waste yarn or stitch holders

Sizing

XS (S, M, L, 1X, 2X, 3X) to fit 71 (81, 92, 102, 112, 122, 132) cm/ 28 (32, 36, 40, 44, 48, 52)" bust with 4cm/1.75" negative ease. Please see schematic for details.

Pattern Notes

This pattern is suitable for experienced knitters.

The cardigan is worked flat and seamlessly bottom-up to the armholes, then the fronts and back are worked separately before

being joined at the shoulders with a three-needle cast-off. The sleeves are worked in the round using a set-in short-row construction. The buttonband and the neckband are worked afterwards.

If a longer cardigan is desired, work additional 12-row repeats before Waist Shaping Rows 1-4 of the rib pattern. If long-waisted, you may wish to add another 12 rows between the two waist-shaping sections. Note you will need more yarn.

You will use 6 stitch markers to help you throughout the body: 2 to mark the outline of the back panel (A), 2 to mark the start of the front panel (one each front; B), 2 to mark the side seams (C). Using three different colours is strongly recommended.

You will also use stitch markers on the sleeves, this time cols A and B. Marker A marks the beg of the rnd, marker B the end of short-row shaping.

INSTRUCTIONS

Set-up

Using smaller needles, CO 129 (149, 169, 189, 209, 229, 249) sts.

Ribbing

Row 1 (RS): p1, work Front Panel Lower Rib, place marker B, (k1, p1) 15 (20, 25, 30, 35, 40, 45) times, place marker A, work Back Panel Lower Rib; place marker A, (p1, k1) 15 (20, 25, 30, 35, 40, 45) times, place marker B, work Front Panel Lower Rib, p1.

Row 2 (WS): k1, work Front Panel Lower Rib, sm B, *p1, k1; rep from * to marker A, sm A, work Back Panel Lower Rib, sm A, *k1, p1; rep from * to marker B, sm B, work Front Panel Lower Rib, k1.

Row 3: p1, work Front Panel Lower Rib, sm B, *k1, p1; rep from * to marker A, sm A, work Back Panel Lower Rib, sm A, *k1, p1; rep from * to marker B, sm B, work Front Panel Lower Rib, p1.

Row 4: k1, work Front Panel Lower Rib, sm B, *p1, k1; rep from * to marker A, sm A, work Back Panel Lower Rib, sm A, *k1, p1; rep from * to marker B, sm B, work Front Panel Lower Rib, k1.

Row 5: p1, work Front Panel Lower Rib, sm B, *k1, p1; rep from * to marker A, sm A, work Back Panel Lower Rib, sm A, *k1, p1; rep from * to marker B, sm B, work

Front Panel Lower Rib, p1.

Row 6: k1, work Front Panel
Lower Rib, sm B, *p1, k1; rep from
* to marker A, sm A, work Back
Panel Lower Rib, sm A, *k1, p1;
rep from * to marker B, sm B,
work Front Panel Lower Rib, k1.

Rep Rows 3-6 another 3 times.
18 rows worked in total.

Change to larger needles.

Body

Row 1 (RS): p1, work Front Panel,
sm B, k12 (17, 22, 27, 32, 37, 42), place
marker C, k to marker A, sm A, work
Back Panel, sm A, k18 (23, 28, 33, 38,
43, 48), place marker C, k to marker
B, sm B, work Front Panel, p1.

Row 2 (WS): k1, work Front Panel,
sm B, p to marker C, sm C, p to
marker A, sm A, work Back Panel, sm
A, p to marker C, sm C, p to marker
B, sm B, work Front Panel, p1.

Each front has 31 (36, 41, 46, 51,
56, 61) sts and the back 67 (77, 87,
97, 107, 117, 127). Fabric between
the panels is worked in st st.

Work even until 1 rep of Front and
Back Panels have been completed.

Work another 0 (0, 6, 6,
6, 6, 6) rows in patt.

Begin Waist Shaping

Shaping Row 1 (RS, dec): p1,
work Front Panel, sm B, k to 3 sts
before marker C, ssk, k1, sm C,
k1, k2tog, k to marker A, sm A,
work Back Panel, sm A, k to 3 sts
before marker C, ssk, k1, sm C, k1,
k2tog, k to marker B, sm B, work
Front Panel, p1. 4 sts decreased.

Shaping Row 2 (WS): k1, work Front
Panel, sm B, p to marker C, sm C, p to
marker A, sm A, work Back Panel, sm
A, p to marker C, sm C, p to marker
B, sm B, work Front Panel, k1.

Shaping Row 3: p1, work Front
Panel, sm B, k to marker A (sm C on
the way), sm A, work Back Panel,
sm A , k to marker B (sm C on the
way), sm B, work Front Panel, p1.

Shaping Row 4: as Row 2.

Work Shaping Rows 1-4 a
total of 3 times. 117 (137, 157,
177, 197, 217, 237) sts

Work even for 12 rows,
ending after a WS row.

Resume Waist Shaping:

Shaping Row 5 (RS, inc): p1, work Front Panel, sm B, k to 1 st before marker C, m1, k1, sm C, k1, m1, k to marker A, sm A, work Back Panel, sm A, k to 1 st before marker C, m1, k1, sm C, k1, m1, k to marker B, sm B, work Front Panel, p1. 4 sts increased.

Shaping Row 6 (WS): k1, work Front Panel, sm B, p to marker C, sm C, p to marker A, sm A, work Back Panel, sm A, p to marker C, sm C, p to marker B, sm B, work Front Panel, k1.

Shaping Row 7: p1, work Front Panel, sm B, k to marker A (sm C on the way), sm A, work Back Panel, sm A, k to marker B (sm C on the way), sm B, work Front Panel, p1.

Shaping Row 8: as Row 6.

Work Shaping Rows 5-8 a total of 3 times. 129 (149, 169, 189, 209, 229, 249) sts

Work even for 17 rows, ending after a RS row.

Divide fronts and back (WS): work to 3 (3, 4, 4, 5, 6, 7) sts before marker C, cast off the next 6 (6, 8, 8, 10, 12, 14) sts (removing marker C), work in patt to 3 (3, 4, 4, 5, 6, 7) sts before next marker C, cast off the next 6

(6, 8, 8, 10, 12, 14) sts (removing marker C), work in patt to end.

28 (33, 37, 42, 46, 50, 54) sts for Right Front, 61 (71, 79, 89, 97, 105, 113) sts for Back, 28 (33, 37, 42, 46, 50, 54) for Left Front. 117 (137, 153, 173, 189, 205, 221) sts Leave Right and Left Front sts on waste yarn or stitch holders.

Back

Rejoin yarn at RH side with RS facing. Start armhole shaping.

Sizes

Size XS

Shaping Row 1 (RS, dec): ssk, work in patt to last 2 sts, k2tog. 59 sts

Shaping Row 2 (WS, dec): p2tog, work in patt to last 2 sts, p2tog tbl. 57 sts

Work Shaping Rows 1 and 2 once more. 53 sts

Shaping Row 3 (RS, dec): as Shaping Row 1. 51 sts

Shaping Row 4 (WS): work in patt to end.

Size S

Shaping Row 1 (RS, dec): cast off

3 sts, work in patt to end. 68 sts

Shaping Row 2 (WS, dec): as
Shaping Row 1. 65 sts

Shaping Row 3 (dec): cast off 2
sts, work in patt to end. 63 sts

Shaping Row 4 (dec): cast off 2 sts,
work in patt to last 2 sts, p2tog. 60 sts

Shaping Row 5 (dec): ssk, work in
patt to last 2 sts, k2tog. 58 sts

Shaping Row 6 (dec): p2tog,
work in patt to end. 57 sts

Sizes M, L, 1X, 2X, and 3X

Shaping Row 1 (RS, dec): ssk,
work in patt to last 2 sts, k2tog.
77 (87, 95, 103, 111) sts

Shaping Row 2 (WS, dec): p2tog,
work in patt to last 2 sts, p2tog
tbl. 75 (85, 93, 101, 109) sts

Work Shaping Rows 1 and
2 another 1 (3, 3, 3, 5) times.
71 (73, 81, 89, 89) sts

Shaping Row 3 (RS, dec):
ssk, work in patt to last 2 sts,
k2tog. 69 (71, 79, 87, 87) sts

Shaping Row 4 (WS):
work in patt to end.

Work Shaping Rows 3 and
4 another 3 (1, 5, 7, 5) times.
63 (69, 69, 73, 77) sts

All Sizes

Work in patt until a total of 42 (42,
48, 48, 56, 60, 60) rows have been
worked from initial armhole cast-off.

Next row (RS): place 9 (9, 11, 13,
13, 15, 17) sts on waste yarn, cast
off 33 (39, 41, 43, 43, 43, 43) sts,
and place rem 9 (9, 11, 13, 13, 15,
17) sts on waste yarn, keeping
both markers A in place.

Right Front

Pick up sts from waste yarn or
stitch holders and rejoin yarn
with RS facing for next row.

Begin armhole shaping.

Size XS

Armhole Shaping Row 1 (RS, dec):
work in patt to last 2 sts, k2tog. 27 sts

Armhole Shaping Row 2 (WS, dec):
p2tog, work in patt to end. 26 sts

Work Armhole Shaping Rows
1 and 2 once more. 24 sts

Armhole Shaping Row 5 (RS, dec):
work in patt to last 2 sts, k2tog. 23 sts

Armhole Shaping Row 6
(WS): work in patt to end.

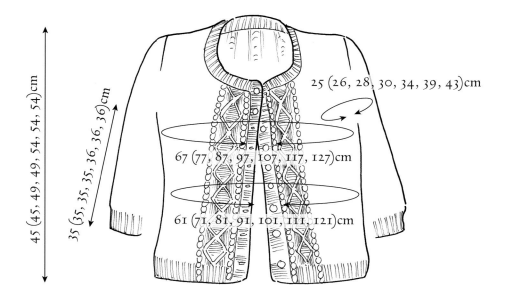

45 (45, 49, 49, 54, 54, 54)cm

35 (35, 35, 35, 36, 36, 36)cm

25 (26, 28, 30, 34, 39, 43)cm

67 (77, 87, 97, 107, 117, 127)cm

61 (71, 81, 91, 101, 111, 121)cm

Size S

Armhole Shaping Row 1 (RS): work in patt to end.

Armhole Shaping Row 2 (WS, dec): cast off 3 sts, work in patt to end. 30 sts

Armhole Shaping Row 3: work in patt to end.

Armhole Shaping Row 4 (dec): cast off 2 sts, work in patt to end. 28 sts

Armhole Shaping Row 5 (dec): work in patt to last 2 sts, k2tog. 27 sts

Armhole Shaping Row 6 (dec): p2tog, work in patt to end. 26 sts

Sizes M, L, 1X, 2X, and 3X

Armhole Shaping Row 1 (RS, dec): work in patt to last 2 sts, k2tog. 36 (41, 45, 49, 53) sts

Armhole Shaping Row 2 (WS, dec): p2tog, work in patt to end. 35 (40, 44, 48, 52) sts

Work Armhole Shaping Rows 1 and 2 another 1 (3, 3, 3, 5) times. 33 (34, 38, 42, 42) sts

Armhole Shaping Row 3 (RS, dec): work in patt to last 2 sts, k2tog. 32 (33, 37, 41, 41) sts

Armhole Shaping Row 4
(WS): work in patt to end.

Work Armhole Shaping Rows
3 and 4 another 3 (1, 5, 7, 5)
times. 29 (32, 32, 34, 36) sts

All Sizes

Begin neckline shaping.

Neckline Shaping Row 1 (RS, dec):
cast off 10 (10, 14, 14, 14, 14, 14)
sts, place marker B and leave it for
rem of shaping, work in patt to
end. 13 (16, 15, 18, 18, 20, 22) sts

Neckline Shaping Row 2
(WS): work in patt to end.

Neckline Shaping Row 3 (RS,
dec): k2tog, work in patt to end.
12 (15, 14, 17, 17, 19, 21) sts

Neckline Shaping Row 4
(WS): work in patt to end.

Work Neckline Shaping Rows 3
and 4 another 3 (6, 3, 4, 4, 4, 4)
times. 9 (9, 11, 13, 13, 15, 17) sts.

Work in patt until a total of 42 (42,
48, 48, 56, 60, 60) rows have been
worked from initial armhole cast-off.

Put rem sts on waste yarn.

Left Front

Pick up sts from waste yarn or
stitch holders and rejoin yarn
with RS facing for next row.

Begin armhole shaping.

Size XS

Armhole Shaping Row 1 (RS, dec):
k2tog, work in patt to end. 27 sts

Armhole Shaping Row 2 (WS, dec):
work in patt to last 2 sts, p2tog. 26 sts

Work Armhole Shaping Rows
1 and 2 once more. 24 sts

Armhole Shaping Row 5 (RS,
dec): as Shaping Row 1. 23 sts

Armhole Shaping Row 6
(WS): work in patt to end.

Size S

Armhole Shaping Row 1
(RS, dec): cast off 3 sts, work
in patt to end. 30 sts

Armhole Shaping Row 2
(WS): work in patt to end.

Armhole Shaping Row 3
(RS, dec): cast off 2 sts, work
in patt to end. 28 sts

Armhole Shaping Row 4

(WS): work in patt to end.

Armhole Shaping Row 5 (RS, dec): k2tog, work in patt to end. 27 sts

Armhole Shaping Row 6 (dec): work in patt to end, p2tog. 26 sts

Sizes M, L, 1X, 2X, and 3X

Armhole Shaping Row 1 (RS, dec): k2tog, work in patt to end. 36 (41, 45, 49, 53) sts

Armhole Shaping Row 2 (WS, dec): work in patt to last 2 sts, p2tog. 35 (40, 44, 48, 52) sts

Work Armhole Shaping Rows 1 and 2 another 1 (3, 3, 3, 5) times. 33 (34, 38, 42, 42) sts

Armhole Shaping Row 3 (RS, dec): k2tog, work in patt to end. 32 (33, 37, 41, 41) sts

Armhole Shaping Row 4 (WS): work in patt to end.

Work Armhole Shaping Rows 3 and 4 another 3 (1, 5, 7, 5) times. 29 (32, 32, 34, 36) sts

All Sizes

Begin neckline shaping.

Neckline Shaping Row 1 (RS, dec):

work in patt to last 10 (10, 14, 14, 14, 14, 14) sts, place marker B and leave it for rem of shaping, cast off rem sts and break yarn. 13 (16, 15, 18, 18, 20, 22) sts

Neckline Shaping Row 2 (WS): rejoin yarn, work in patt to end.

Neckline Shaping Row 3 (dec): k2tog, work in patt to end. 12 (15, 14, 17, 17, 19, 21) sts

Neckline Shaping Row 4 (WS): work in patt to end.

Work Neckline Shaping Rows 3 and 4 another 3 (6, 3, 4, 4, 4, 4) times. 9 (9, 11, 13, 13, 15, 17) sts.

Work in patt until a total of 42 (42, 48, 48, 56, 60, 60) rows have been worked from initial armhole cast-off.

Put rem sts on waste yarn.

Joining Shoulders

Work a three-needle cast-off on each shoulder as specified in Special Techniques, page 130.

Sleeves

Starting at the centre of the underarm cast-off and using larger needles, pick up and k3 (3, 4, 4, 5, 6, 6) sts from underarm cast-off, k6 (6, 8, 8, 10, 12, 14) sts along armhole shaping, k48 along rest of the arm-scye, k6 (6, 8, 8, 10, 12, 14) sts along armhole shaping, and k3 (3, 4, 4, 5, 6, 6) sts from underarm cast-off, place marker C to mark beg of rnd and join in the rnd. 66 (66, 72, 72, 78, 84, 88) sts

Short Row 1: k9 (9, 12, 12, 15, 18, 20), place marker D, k29, w&t.

Short Row 2: p10, w&t.

Short Row 3: k11, w&t.

Continue to work short rows, working 1 st more each row until the last st before marker D is wrapped.

Next Short Row: knit.

Resume working in the rnd, removing marker D, and start decreasing at the underarm.

Underarm Decrease Rnd: k1, k2tog, k to 3 sts before end, ssk, k1. 64 (64, 70, 70, 76, 82, 86) sts

Work Underarm Decrease Rnd as established, decreasing 2 sts every rnd, a total of 7 (6, 7, 4, 3, 1, 0) times. 50 (52, 56, 62, 70, 80, 86) sts

Knit 5 rnds.

Begin sleeve shaping.

Next Rnd (dec): k1, k2tog, k to

3 sts before end, ssk, k1. sm. 48 (50, 54, 60, 68, 78, 84) sts

Work this decrease rnd every 14th (16th, 16th, 14th, 10th, 8th, 8th) rnd, 1 (3, 3, 1, 8, 8, 5) times total. 46 (44, 48, 58, 52, 62, 74) sts

Then work this decrease rnd every 12th (12th, 12th, 12th, 8th, 6th, 6th) rnd, 5 (2, 2, 5, 0, 3, 7) times. 36 (40, 44, 48, 52, 56, 60) sts

Knit 3 rnds.

Change to smaller needles.

Rib Row: *k1, p1; rep from * to end.

Rep Rib Row another 6 times.

Cast off: p1, *p1, pass first worked st over second worked st; rep from * to end.

Neckband

Starting at Right Front with RS facing and using smaller needles, pick up and k7 (7, 9, 9, 9, 9, 9) sts from cast-off edge to marker B, remove marker B, pick up and k24 (26, 26, 26, 26, 26, 26) sts to marker A, remove marker A, pick up and k21 across the 31-st Back Panel, remove marker A, pick up and k24 (26, 26, 26, 26, 26, 26) sts to marker

B, remove marker B, pick up and k7 (7, 9, 9, 9, 9, 9) sts from cast-off edge. 83 (87, 91, 91, 91, 91, 91) sts

Rib Row 1 (WS): k1, *p1, k1; rep from * to end.

Rib Row 2 (RS): p1, *k1, p1; rep from * to end.

Work in patt for a total of 9 rows.

Cast off pwise on RS.

Buttonband

Right buttonband:

Starting at the bottom RH edge with RS facing and using smaller needles, pick up and k57 (57, 65, 65, 73, 73, 73) sts.

Rib Row 1 (WS): p1, *k1, p1; rep from * to last st.

Rib Row 2 (RS): k1, *p1, k1; rep from * to end.

Rep Rib Rows 1 and 2 once more, then Row 1 again.

Buttonhole Row (RS): Work 4

sts in patt, then *p2tog, yo, work 6 sts in patt; rep from * another 5 (5, 6, 6, 7, 7, 7) times, p2tog, yo, work 3 sts in pattern.

Work another 5 rows in rib as est.

Cast off pwise on RS.

Left buttonband

Starting at the top LH edge with RS facing and using smaller needles, pick up and k57 (57, 65, 65, 73, 73, 73) sts.

Rib Row 1 (WS): p1, *k1, p1; rep from * to last st.

Rib Row 2 (RS): k1, *p1, k1; rep from * to end. 11

Rep Rows 1 and 2 another 5 times, then Row 1 again.

Cast off pwise on RS.

Finishing

Noting placement of buttonholes, sew on buttons. Weave in ends.

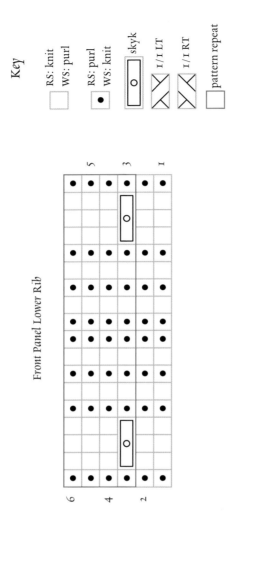

Key

RS: knit
WS: purl

RS: purl
WS: knit

skyk

1/1 LT

1/1 RT

pattern repeat

Front Panel Lower Rib

Back Panel Lower Rib

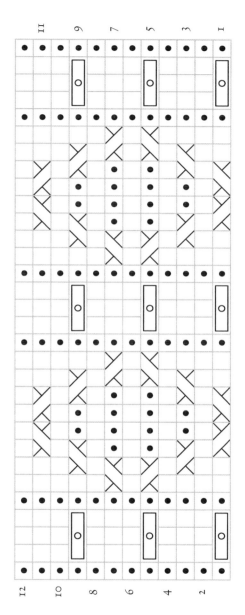

Back Panel

Front Panel

2.2

INVENTION

MAJUSCULE & MINUSCULE

Upper and lower case letters.

The seas of experience / That were so broad and deep / So immediate and sleep /
Are suddenly still / You may say what you will / At such peace I am terrified.

T. S. ELIOT
Silence, 1909

I have a complex relationship with the idea of tradition. I keep wondering how something becomes tradi tional and who can truly lay claim to a tradition. I am acutely aware of these questions within my own work as a knitwear designer and a tutor. From being told I cannot knit a traditional Fair Isle jumper because I am not from Shetland, to encountering strong opinions about Nordic knitting traditions from non-Nordic people, I am intrigued by the idea of a fixed, unalterable tradition.

The word 'tradition' is derived from a Latin verb—*tradere* or *tra-derere*—which means 'to hand over' or 'to give over for safe-keeping'. While the etymological roots may feel reassuringly tactile to crafters reading this (many of you are probably imagining a well-loved jumper being handed down from generation to generation), it strikes me that the etymology also suggests a tradition is not a static thing; a tradition is forever slowly changing as we leave our own traces upon it.

What does it mean when we assign fixed identities to knitting conventions; believing colourwork can only be stranded across three stitches and have two colours per row? What does it mean when knitting traditions and knitting heritage are overlaid with nostalgia, romanticism and (occasionally) a dash of Othering? What happens when we celebrate traditions as something to imitate and recapture through so-called 'correct' techniques and materials? How does it work when someone lays claim to a tradition?

Through my work with both book history and knitting, I have come to realise that nothing is fixed-in-time-and-place. I have long been fascinated by Gutenberg's invention of the printing press precisely because while we may believe that it caused the world to shift on its axis overnight, the real story is far more complex. The earliest books were nearly impossible to distinguish from manuscripts and often hand-finished by artisans who continued to also work on manuscripts. In fact, this particular pattern is inspired by some of the ornamentation in early printed books. I wanted to pick up on the many combinations of patterns and colours so freely scattered across the pages. Just like today when an ebook device is being marketed as 'paperwhite', there was a desire and need to claim legitimacy by modelling new technology on old, and printers designed typefaces that mimicked handwriting.

Things change. They always do. And yet we humans will always tell stories that make sense of ever-changing things. Stories are what make us humans.

What stories do we tell about knitting? I think it depends upon who we are.

I like to think of how motifs and

knitting styles travel as much as languages and stories. Knitting designer Liz Lovick from Orkney, has long been documenting the recurrent use of lace motifs in such geographically distant places as Iceland and Estonia. The much-loved Shetland XO motif appeared on the famous Faroese jumper in the Nordic Noir TV series, The Killing in 2007. Tree and anchor motifs are continuously interpreted in texture, lace, and colourwork depending upon which regional knitting style you examine.

There are several ways of looking at and using knitting traditions. In early 2017 the fashion house Alexander McQueen used traditional Shetland lace knitting in its collection. Using traditional knitting to signal aspirational slow-fashion and authentically British, it promoted itself as equally aspirational slow-fashion and authentically British. The label's frequent use of so-called 'heritage crafts' creates a continual and deliberate tension between high fashion and presumed rustic making.

Knitting traditions can also be used as a narrative device. In The Killing,

detective Sarah Lund immediately stands out as The Girl In The Woolly Jumper in a sea of suits. Lund's jumper is a rustic woolly jumper, clearly handmade, and steeped in Nordic traditions and iconography. We do not need an introduction to Sarah Lund. The jumper has already told us her story, her landscape, her personality.

Finally, knitters have their own stories about knitting traditions. I have lost count of how many times I have been told the story of how Aran cables and stitches were family- or community-specific, so that the patterned jumpers could be used to identify drowned fishermen. It is a persuasive story that sees knitting as text as well as textile, but sadly it is untrue. Likewise, I have heard many claims that one particular stitch pattern was invented in a certain village or that certain colourwork patterns are more traditional than others. Knitting traditional items can be a way of expressing kinship or interest in a location. It can also be a way of claiming authenticity.

I always ask who has the authority to decide that something knitted in

1900 is more traditional than something knitted in 1950 or 2000? How can we fix things in time so decisively? I offer the notion that a monolithic, solid knitting tradition is problematic as it cannot be forever unalterable and fixed-in-time-and-place. Designers, writers, and knitters keep mixing and remixing 'traditional' patterns and what they mean to us. We find it difficult to pin the idea of 'tradition' down because the idea itself carries an internal battle of competing signifiers—or connotations, if you like—and this battle of signifiers will never be resolved.

Knitting traditions will continue to evolve, change, and shift as long as there are knitters to tell new stories. ☞

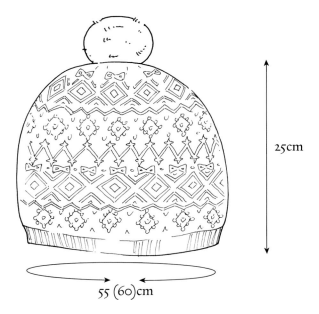

25cm

55 (60)cm

MAJUSCULE & MINUSCULE
HAT & FINGERLESS MITTS

🐦

Materials

Blacker Swan Falkland Islands
4-ply (4ply; 175m/190yds
per 50g ball; 100% wool)

2 balls in Pale Maiden (A)

1 ball each in Sky Grey (B),
Hawkweed (C), Tussac (D)
and Mountain Berry (E)

Needles Used

For smaller size of hat
or fingerless mitts:

2.75mm/US 2, DPNs or preferred
needles for small circumferences

3.5mm/US 4, DPNs or preferred
needles for small circumferences

For larger size of hat or
fingerless mitts:

3mm/US 3, DPNs or preferred
needles for small circumferences

3.75mm/US 4, DPNs or preferred
needles for small circumferences

Gauge

For smaller size: 26 sts x 28
rows = 10cm x 10cm / 4" x 4"
measured over blocked colourwork
on 3.5mm/US 4 needles

For larger size: 24 sts x 26 rows =
10cm x 10cm / 4" x 4" measured
over blocked colourwork on
3.75mm/ US 4 needles

Accessories

Stitch holder

Waste yarn

Sizing

Hat: S/M and L/XL to fit 55 and 60 cm / 22 and 24" head circumference

Fingerless mitts: S/M and L/XL to fit 18.5 and 20 cm / 7.25" and 8" hand circumference

Pattern Notes

This pattern is suitable for intermediate knitters.

The hat and the fingerless mitts are all worked in the round using stranded knitting.

The hat has a very slouchy fit. If a less slouchy fit is desired, start working Chart A on Rnd 11.

The fingerless mitts have a tight fit. If you have a relatively large wrist or forearm compared to your hand, opt for the size up.

Note on yarn: Swan 4ply is a heavy 4ply and the fabric has a great deal of drape. If you prefer a denser fabric, use the Blacker Swan Falkland Islands DK knitted at gauge as specified above.

INSTRUCTIONS

Hat

Using col A and smaller

needles, cast on 120 sts.

Join to work in the round, being careful not to twist. Pm to mark beg of rnd.

Rnd 1: *k1, p1; rep from * to end.

Rep Rnd 1 another 9 times.

Change to larger needles.

Next Rnd (inc): *k4, m1, k1; rep from * to end. 144 sts.

Next Rnd: knit.

Rnds 1-33: work Chart A once.

Rnds 34-61: work Chart B once. 24 sts

Next Rnd (dec): k2tog to end. 12 sts

Break yarn and thread through rem sts. Pull tight to fasten.

Fingerless Mitts

Using col A and smaller needles, cast on 48 sts.

Join to work in the rnd, being careful not to twist. Pm to mark beg of rnd.

Rnd 1: *k1, p1; rep from * to end.

Rep Rnd 1 another 14 times.

Change to larger needles.

Next Rnd: knit.

Rnds 1-33: work Chart A once.

Rnds 34-54: work Chart C once.

Place 19 sts on to waste
yarn (for the thumb).

Rnds 55-57: work Chart D once.

Next Rnd: using col A, knit.

Change to smaller needles.

Next Rnd: *k1, p1; rep from * to end.

Rep last rnd another 4 times.

Cast off in patt.

Thumb Gusset

Carefully remove the waste yarn
and, using col A and larger needles,
pick up and knit 19 thumb sts, 1
st from side of gusset, 1 st from
top of gusset, and 1 st from
other side of gusset. 22 sts

Pm to mark beg of rnd.

Change to smaller needles.

Rnd 1: *k1, p1; rep from * to end.

Rep Rnd 1 another 4 times.

Cast off in patt.

Make 2 fingerless mitts alike.

Finishing

Weave in ends, but do not trim.

Use lengths of yarn to close any gaps
surrounding the thumb gusset area.

Steam block gently to even
out colourwork.

Once dry, trim ends.

Make a 5cm/2" pompom in col A.
Secure it to the top of the hat.

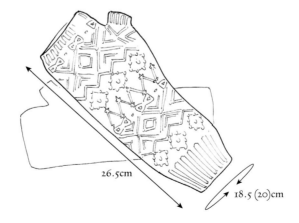

26.5cm

18.5 (20)cm

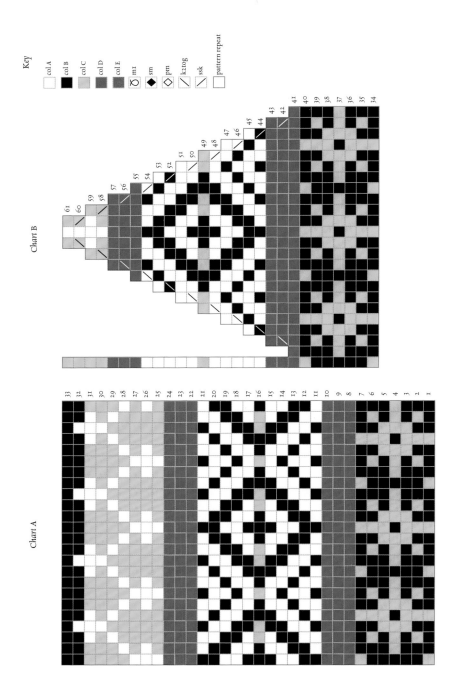

Key

Chart B

Chart A

Chart C

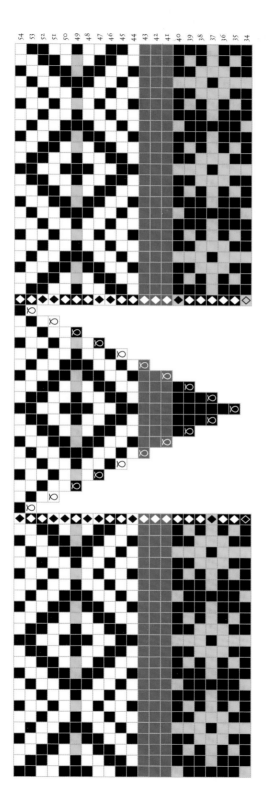

Chart D

2.3

INVENTION

—————— ·•· ——————

LETTERPRESS

A method of printing in which raised surfaces covered with ink are pressed onto paper.

—————— ·•· ——————

A river is more than an amenity, it is a treasure.

OLIVER WENDELL HOLMES, JR

⁊☙

I arrived in Mainz, Germany one winter evening in 2016 when it was too dark to see anything from my small hotel window except the neon lights from the nearby supermarket. The next morning I got up early and walked down to the Rhine river, flowing just a few hundred metres beyond the concrete and neon signs. The sunrise was refracted through the morning fog and gave the eastern banks of the river a yellow tinge. I thought of ancient civilisations and important cities growing up along rivers. Our modern-day eyes are trained to see rivers as obstacles which we travel over in cars or trains, but rivers were the original superhighways, patient conveyors of commerce and gatherers of knowledge.

As I sat by the Rhine with my

morning coffee, I began thinking of the changes that Gutenberg's invention of the printing press brought about and what it must have been like living at that time.

Once, books were the dominion of the powerful people in society, but the printing press allowed for dissenting voices to spread quicker and wider. Smarter people than I would tell you about how texts from antiquity were rediscovered by the Italian Renaissance to the south and then, thanks to the invention of the printing press, disseminated throughout Europe, leading to scientific breakthroughs, advances in philosophy, and eventually to the Enlightenment.

They would tell you about Martin Luther's Reformation, the discovery of the Americas, Leonardo da Vinci's studies of human anatomy, and the end of feudalism and the subsequent rise of mercantilism. You would hear stories about the end of the Middle Ages and the beginning of the Early Modern era. Grand tales. Some book historians like to use phrases such as the printing revolution but I am slightly more cautious. The

changes were slow and continuous and persistent.

As I was sitting there, by the Rhine, in the morning fog with my *Tasse Kaffee* and with Mainz waking up around me, I began wondering if things are so different nowadays.

I know that Gutenberg's first Bible was printed around 1455. Fifty years later vernacular languages had been given legitimacy by print, as commercially there was a bigger audience if a book was written in a language understood by most people (printing drove much of the rise of the vernacular languages throughout Europe: the first book in German was printed in 1461, Italian in 1470, Spanish in 1472, English in 1475, French and Greek in 1476, and so forth. Only a small number of incunabula used vernacular languages but they were important). Scientific discoveries, major societal changes, dissenting voices (Martin Luther, Galileo Galilei, Nicolaus Copernicus, among many others)—are all these things so very different to what has happened to us with the internet? These days so many people work in jobs that did not exist twenty-five years ago and we have a US president who spends a lot of time tweeting (how would you have described tweeting twenty-five years ago? Social media? YouTube stars? Cloud architects? SEO experts? *Political doge memes?*).

This very book takes its name from a treatise written by Johannes Trithemius. His *In Praise of Scribes* is one long and steady diatribe about how print is a modern fad that will soon disappear while the work of scribes endures. Ironically the manuscript version of Trithemius's work has not survived, but we still have a printed version from 1494. It reads very much like a lengthy opinion piece penned by an old man about the evils of the radio or the TV or the internet. *Plus ça change, plus c'est la même chose.*

I finished my drink and walked away from the river, that first conduit of communication and knowledge, and walked towards the Gutenberg Museum and its printing presses checking my e-mails on my phone. Three eras of communication and information technology—and all before my second cup of coffee.

Sweet Rhine, run softly. ☞

LETTERPRESS COWL

Materials

Blacker Yarns British Classic
Aran (aran-weight; 70m/76 yds
per 50g ball; 100% wool)

4 balls

Sample shown in Natural Fawn

Needles Used

4.5mm/US 7, circular, 60cm/24"

5.5mm/US 9, circular, 60cm/24"

Gauge

17 sts x 26 rows = 10cm x
10cm / 4" x 4" measured over
pattern on larger needles

Accessories

Stitch marker

Sizing

One size; 70cm by 34 cm / 27.5"
by 13.25". Please see pattern notes
for sizing modifications.

Pattern Notes

This pattern is suitable for
intermediate knitters.

The cowl is worked in the
round on circular needles.

The cable stitches used do not
require a cable needle.

Note that the cowl as written
uses very close to all 4 balls.
Check your gauge carefully.
If you are a loose knitter, you
may need an additional ball.

For larger cowl with circumference
of 99cm/39", cast on 168 sts and

continue in patt. Note that you will need more yarn if doing so.

INSTRUCTIONS

Using smaller needles, cast on 120 sts. Join to work in the rnd, being careful not to twist. Pm to mark beg of rnd.

Rib

Rnd 1: k1, *p1, k2; rep from * to last 2 sts, p1, k1.

Rep Rnd 1 another 9 times.

Change to larger needles and knit 1 rnd.

Cable Section

Working in patt from chart or written instructions, work Chart A twice (64 rnds in total).

Work Rnds 1-3 of Chart A once.

Change to smaller needles.

Work Rib rnd 10 times in total.

Cast off loosely.

Written Instructions

Rnd 1: *p2, k2, p2; rep from * to end.

Rnd 2: *k2, 1/1 LT, k4, 1/1

RT, k2; rep from * to end.

Rnds 3, 5 and 7: as Rnd 1.

Rnd 4: knit.

Rnd 6: as Rnd 2.

Rnd 8: *k3, 1/1 LT, k2, 1/1 RT, k3; rep from * to end.

Rnd 9: *[p2, k3] twice, p2; rep from * to end.

Rnd 10: *k4, 1/1 LT, 1/1 RT, k4; rep from * to end.

Rnds 11 and 13: *p2, k8, p2; rep from * to end.

Rnd 12: *k5, 1/1 RT, k5; rep from * to end

Rnd 14: *k4, 1/1 RT, 1/1 LT, k4; rep from * to end.

Rnd 15: as Rnd 9.

Rnd 16: *k3, 1/1 RT, k2, 1/1 LT, k3; rep from * to end.

Rnd 17: *p2, k2, p2; rep from * to end.

Rnd 18: as Rnd 2.

Rnds 19, 21 and 23: as Rnd 17.

Rnd 20: knit.

Rnd 22: as Rnd 2

Rnd 24: *k9, 1/1 LT, k2, 1/1 RT, k9; rep from * to end.

Rnd 25: *p2, k2, p4, k3, p2, k3, p4, k2, p2; rep from * to end.

Rnd 26: *k10, 1/1 LT, 1/1 RT, k10; rep from * to end.

Rnd 27: *p2, k2, p4, k8, p4, k2, p2; rep from * to end

Rnd 28: *k11, 1/1 RT, k11;

rep from * to end.

Rnd 29: as Rnd 27.

Rnd 30: *k10, 1/1 RT, 1/1 LT, k10; rep from * to end.

Rnd 31: as Rnd 25.

Rnd 32: *k9, 1/1 RT, k2, 1/1 LT, k9; rep from * to end.

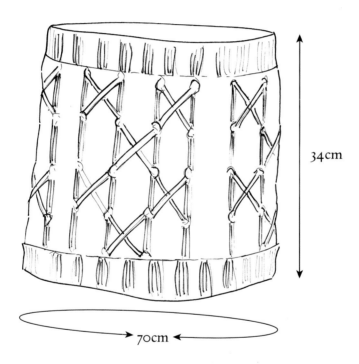

34cm

70cm

Chart A

Key

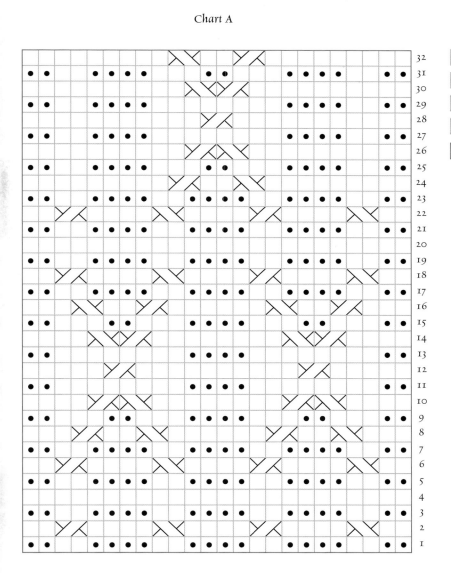

knit

• purl

1/1 LT

1/1 RT

pattern repeat

2.4

INVENTION

RUBRICATION

The he act of arranging, writing or printing red letters.

Having been an early admirer of the beauty of letters, I became insensibly desirous of contributing to the perfection of them.

JOHN BASKERVILLE

T he Rubrication shawl was the first pattern I designed for *This Thing of Paper* and, in its own way, is the very reason this book exists. Its stitch pattern resembles nibs spilling ink across a surface and droplets becoming leaves (we often refer to a leaf of paper, of course). It is a pattern which is both text and texture.

When we look at manuscripts and early printed books with modern eyes, rubricated letters look beautiful. We admire the artistic expression and connect both with the beauty of the red letters and the underlying human hand. These manuscripts and books are treasured as decorative objects rather than as texts to read.

And yet the decorative elements we

admire are actually used with purpose. The red letters were used to add emphasis (like our italics or underlined letters) or to give structure to a block of text (like our chapter headings or paragraph breaks). Readers understood the red letters as a way of guiding their reading: key passages in medieval manuscripts were rendered in red, instructions were underlined in red ink, and red initials flagged sections and new paragraphs.

Gutenberg tried to continue the practice of rubrication and initially headings were printed in red. It was a complex process and each page had to be printed twice, first in black, then in red, which added cost to the production. Soon printers simply left spaces for rubrication to be added by hand. The early printed books were not yet fully mechanised: scribes were still needed to finish them. This was both a continuation of how books were read and understood, and a technical limitation.

We tend to think of writing as making ideas permanent, and of printed books as possessing authority. Yet rubrication differs from manuscript to manuscript and from book to book. Obviously some aspects of a text would always be deemed important and worthy of distinction (specific prayer instructions, for example), but often rubricators would interpret the text in their own ways and add emphasis to different things. Sometimes rubrication was added on top of printed elements, quite counter to what the printer may have planned. Each individual copy was a meeting of, or dialogue between, a clean copy and someone responding to the text. While you can still find traces of rubrication instructions in the margins of a manuscript ('this section needs to be highlighted'), the rubricators were able to offer their own interpretations of the text. The 'true meaning' of a book would be filtered and interpreted through the work of several hands before arriving in front of the reader. And yet it was expected by the reader.

Technological advances such as the invention of italic typefaces around 1500 (claimed to have been invented by the Venetian humanist Aldus Manutius, who also laid claim to formalising the use of the semi-colon; what a legacy!) and printers' decisions to centralise production meant that the book turned from a multicoloured object into a mono-chrome object. Fewer voices were present on the page.

I had very specific aesthetic reasons why I wanted this shawl to form a central part of my book (and I spent a long time looking at yarn dyers before finding the perfect red yarn), but

I had another consideration too. As a knitwear designer, I love seeing how different knitters interpret my pat-terns and my heart bursts with joy when I see someone taking my pat-tern somewhere I could never have imagined. My pattern is always just a starting point and I take great pride in having knitters add their own voices. Rubricators to my own text.

So, dear knitter, this one is in hon-our of you. ☞

RUBRICATION SHAWL

Materials

Travelknitter Tanami (4ply;
400m/435yds per 100g skein;
50% baby camel/50% silk)

2 skeins

Sample shown in Double Happiness

Needles Used

3.75mm/US 5, circular, 80cm/32"

Gauge

21 sts x 30 rows = 10cm x 10cm / 4" x
4" measured over blocked lace patt

Sizing

One size: 168cm (upper edge) by
103cm (side) by 178 cm (lower
edge) / 66" (upper edge) by 40.5"
(side) by 70" (lower edge)

Pattern Notes

This pattern is suitable for
experienced knitters.

This is an asymmetrical shawl that
is shaped by adding two new sts
on the right-hand side of every
RS row. The left-hand side has a
four-row lace edging but continues
straight, whilst the right-hand
side grows quickly (and eventually
becomes the top edge). The stitch
patterns are worked straight on your
needles, but will appear to be at an
angle once you wear the shawl.

Take time to check your gauge as
it is important to this project.

INSTRUCTIONS

Cast on 8 sts.

Next Row: Knit.

Rows 1-48: work Chart A once. 56 sts

Rows 49-208: work Chart B
four times. 216 sts

Rows 209-244: work Chart B
stopping at Chart Row 84. 252 sts

Rows 245-288: work
Chart C once. 296 sts

Cast off as foll: k2, *put both
sts back onto LH needle, k2tog
tbl, k1; rep from* until end.

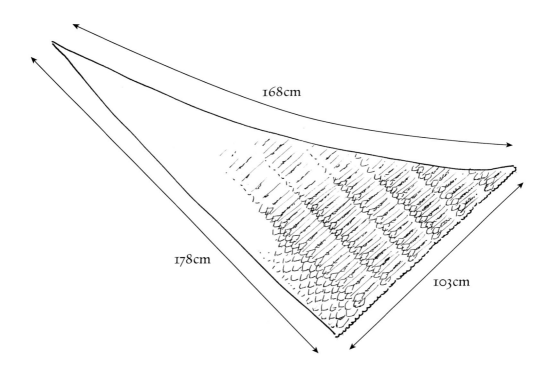

168cm

178cm

103cm

Chart A

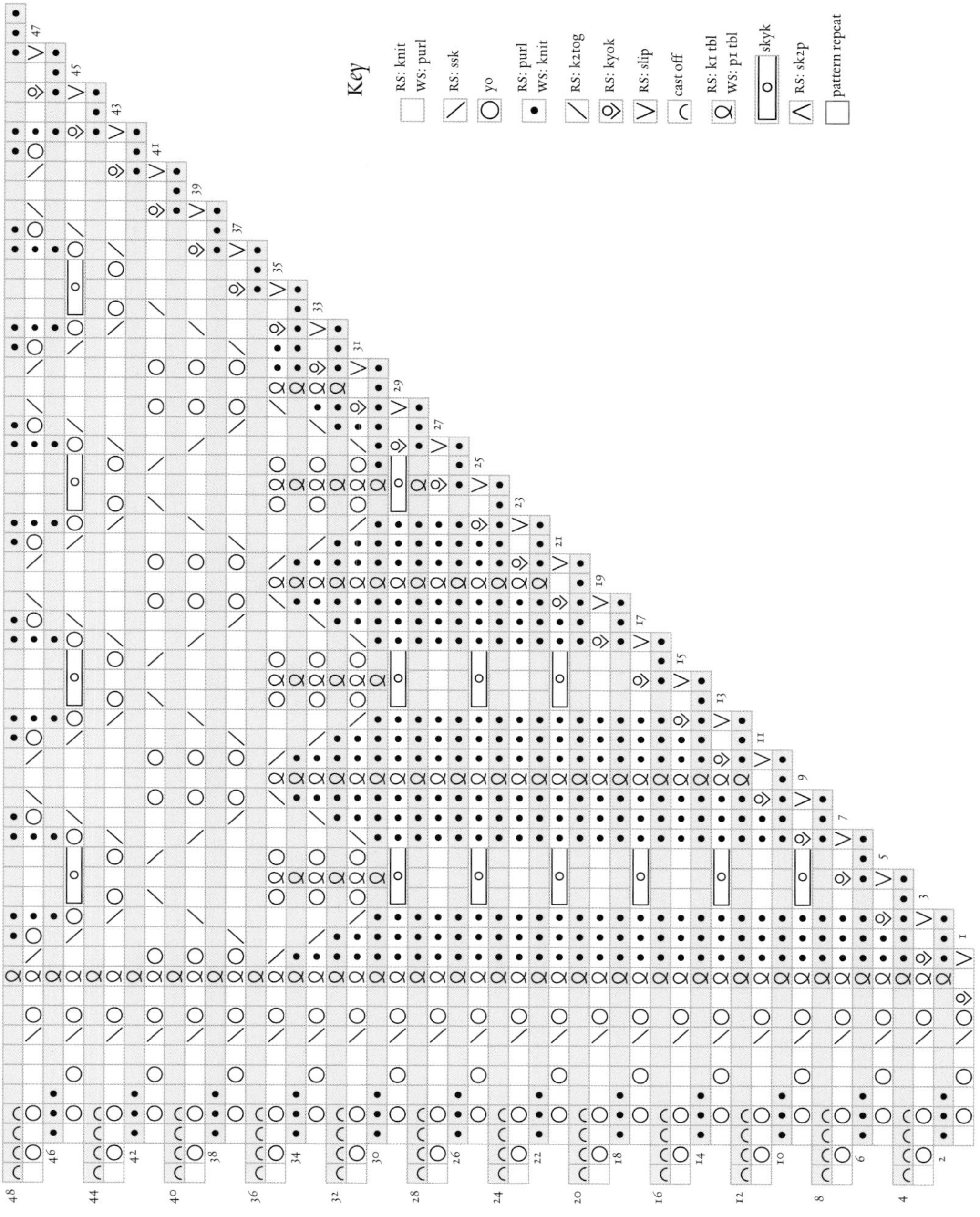

Key

□	RS: knit / WS: purl
╱	RS: ssk
○	yo
●	RS: purl / WS: knit
╱	RS: k2tog
◇	RS: kyok
∨	RS: slip
⌒	cast off
Ǫ	RS: kr tbl / WS: p1 tbl
▯ (with ○)	skyk
⋁	RS: sk2p
□	pattern repeat

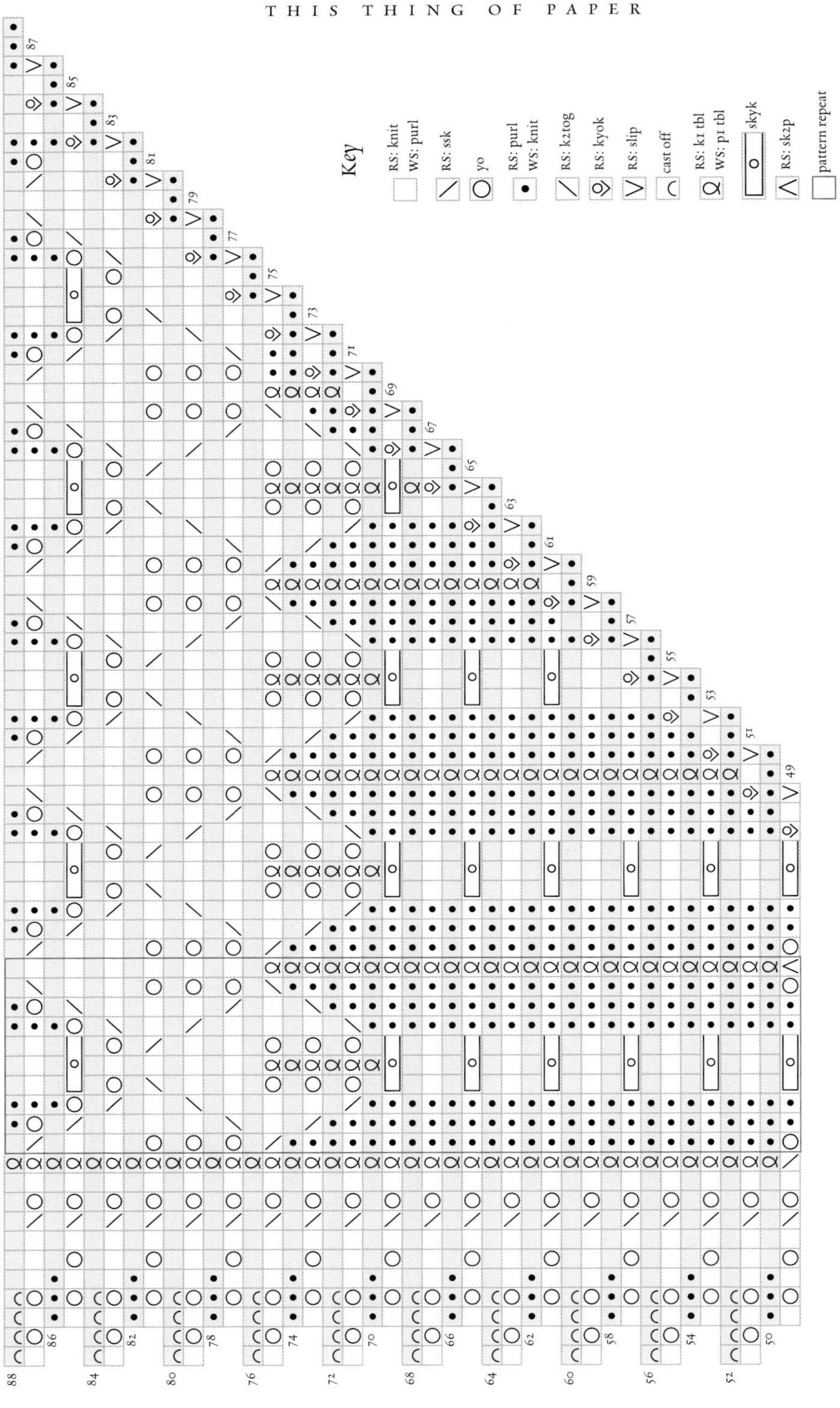

Chart B

Key

RS: knit / WS: purl

RS: ssk

yo

RS: purl / WS: knit

RS: k2tog

RS: kyok

RS: slip

cast off

RS: k1 tbl / WS: p1 tbl

skyk

RS: sk2p

pattern repeat

Chart C

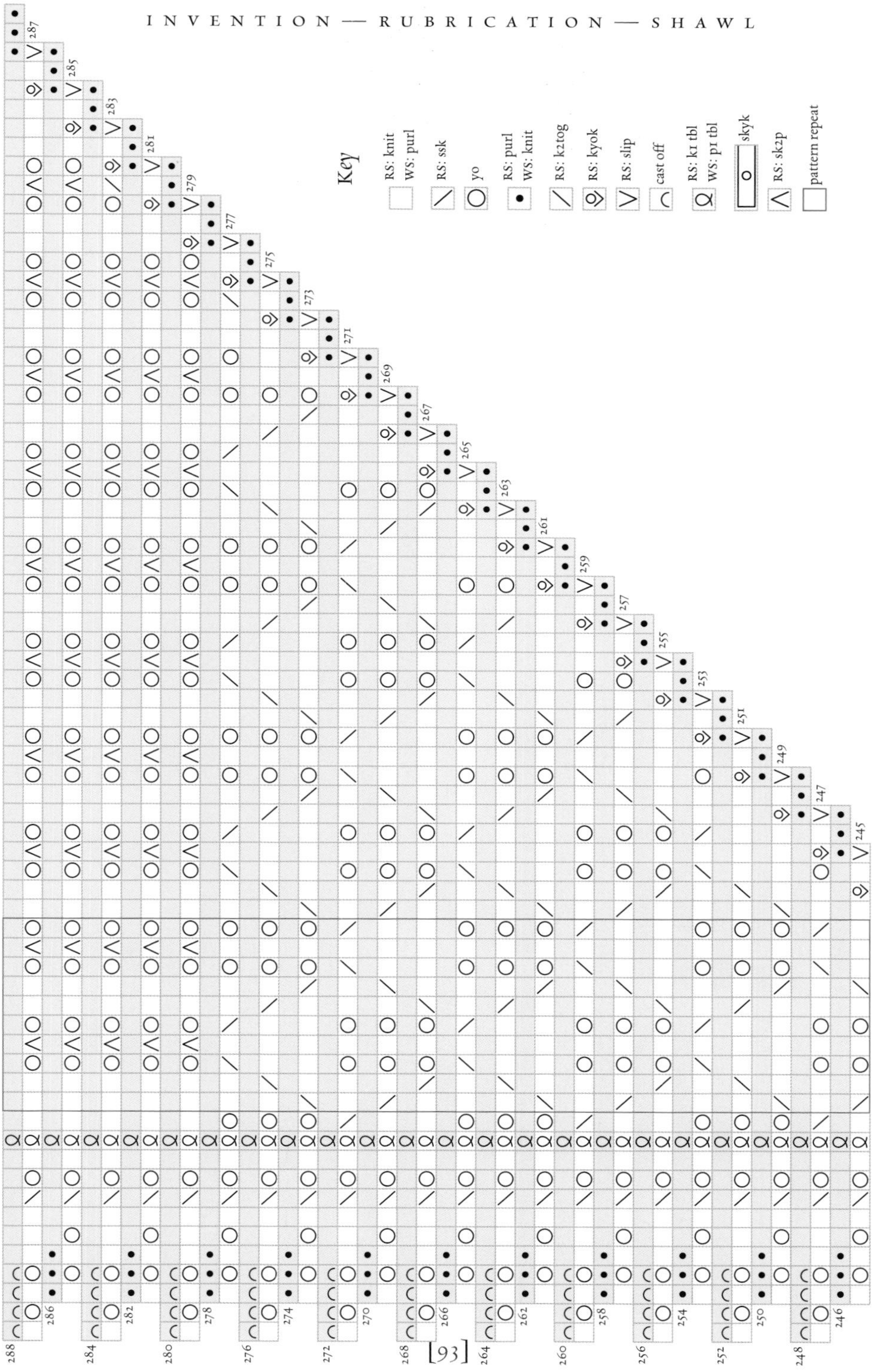

Key

□	RS: knit / WS: purl
╱	RS: ssk
○	yo
•	RS: purl / WS: knit
╱	RS: k2tog
⊘	RS: kyok
⋁	RS: slip
⌒	cast off
Ⓠ	RS: k1 tbl / WS: p1 tbl
○	skyk
⋀	RS: sk2p
□	pattern repeat

3.1
PRINTED

---•---

MARGINALIA
Marks made in the margins of a book.

---•---

There are books in which the footnotes, or the comments scrawled by some reader's hand in the margin, are more interesting than the text. The world is one of these books.

GEORGE SANTAYANA

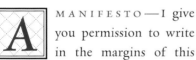

MANIFESTO—I give you permission to write in the margins of this book. Mark your spot and write your own commentary. Circle the size you are knitting or underline the passages that annoy you. Go ahead. You are allowed. A book is never finished and is always in dialogue with you, dear reader.

I give you permission to write in the margins of your knitting. Make your mark by slipping stitches and watch the colour changes flow. Use the stitches as you would use words. Use your yarn as ink. Go ahead. You are allowed. A knitting project is never finished: as you cast off, the project changes character and becomes something worn. It is always in dialogue with its wearer and its knitter.

Deface with joy and do so thoughtfully. Disrupt and ask questions — especially when you are told you cannot. Go make your mark. You are needed.

Making stuff is powerful. Making stuff gives you agency. Making stuff transforms. Making stuff makes something out of nothing. Go make stuff. ☞

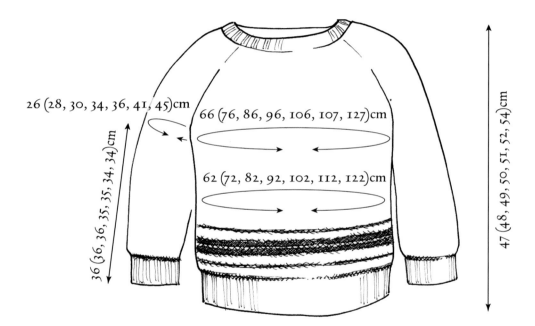

26 (28, 30, 34, 36, 41, 45)cm

66 (76, 86, 96, 106, 107, 127)cm

62 (72, 82, 92, 102, 112, 122)cm

36 (36, 36, 35, 35, 34, 34)cm

47 (48, 49, 50, 51, 52, 54)cm

MARGINALIA JUMPER

Materials

Blacker Yarns Lyonesse DK (DK;
109m / 119 yds per 50g ball; 50% wool
(Corriedale and Merino), 50% linen)

8 (8, 8, 9, 9, 10, 11) balls
in Moonstone (A)

1 (1, 1, 2, 2, 3, 3) balls
in Serpentine (B)

Needles Used

3.75mm / US 5, DPNs or preferred
needles for small circumferences

3.75mm / US 5, circular, 80cm / 32"

4mm / US 6, DPNs or preferred
needles for small circumferences

4mm / US 6, circular, 80cm / 32"

Gauge

20 sts x 29 rows = 10cm x 10cm
/ 4" x 4" measured over blocked
st st on larger needles

Accessories

4 stitch markers

Waste yarn

Tapestry needle

Sizing

XS (S, M, L, 1X, 2X, 3X) to fit 71
(81, 91, 101, 111, 122, 132)cm /
28 (32, 36, 40, 44, 48, 52)" bust
with 5 cm / 2" of negative ease.
Please see schematic for details.

Pattern Notes

This pattern is suitable for
adventurous beginner /
intermediate knitters.

This jumper is worked top-
down in the round with a
slip-stitch pattern feature.

Owing to the nature of the yarn,
the jumper has been designed with

some negative ease, as the yarn will relax over time. If substituting with a different yarn blend, consider the drape of the fabric when deciding which size to knit. If the swatch is particularly firm even at the specified gauge, consider choosing a size up.

Please see Special Techniques, page 131, for GSR (German short row).

INSTRUCTIONS

Yoke

Using smaller needles and col A, cast on 116 (124, 136, 144, 152, 160, 160) sts, join to knit in the rnd, taking care not to twist.

Rib Rnd: *k2, p2; rep from * to end.

Work Rib Rnd another 8 times.

Change to larger needles. Now divide sts into Right Sleeve, Front, Left Sleeve, and Back.

Set-up Rnd: k20 (20, 22, 22, 22, 24, 24), pm, k38 (42, 46, 50, 54, 56, 56), pm, k20 (20, 22, 22, 22, 24, 24), pm, k38 (42, 46, 50, 54, 56, 56), pm.

Raise Back

Short Row 1 (RS): k to third marker,

k19 (21, 23, 25, 27, 28, 28), m1, k until 5 sts from end, turn. 1 st increased.

Short Row 2 (WS): work GSR Right Side, p to 5 sts from marker, turn.

Short Row 3 (RS): work GSR Wrong Side, k to 5 sts from distorted/doubled st, turn.

Short Row 4 (WS): work GSR Right Side, p to 5 sts from distorted/doubled st, turn.

Short Row 5 (RS): work GSR Wrong Side, k to end, working distorted/doubled sts as you find them.

Begin Raglan Shaping

Yoke Rnd 1 (inc): *kfb, k to 1 st from marker, kfb, sm; rep from * another 3 times. 8 sts increased

Yoke Rnd 2: knit, slipping all markers.

Work Yoke Rnds 1 and 2 a total of 20 (20, 22, 26, 28, 34, 38) times. 277 (285, 313, 353, 377, 433, 465) sts

Divide for Body and Sleeves

Next Rnd: place 60 (60, 66, 74, 78, 92, 100) sts on waste yarn, cast on 4

(4, 4, 4, 4, 6, 6) sts, remove marker, k78 (82, 90, 102, 110, 124, 132), remove marker, place 60 (60, 66, 74, 78, 92, 100) sts on waste yarn, remove marker, cast on 2 (2, 2, 2, 2, 3, 3) sts, pm for side seam, cast on (2, 2, 2, 2, 3, 3) sts, k79 (83, 91, 103, 111, 125, 133), remove marker. 165 (173, 189, 213, 229, 261, 277) sts

Next Rnd: k2 (2, 2, 2, 2, 2, 2) sts and pm for new beg of rnd.

Body

Work even for 20 (20, 22, 22, 24, 24, 26) rnds.

Waist Shaping

Shaping Rnd 1 (dec): *k1, k2tog, k to 3 sts from marker, ssk, k1, sm; rep from * once more. 161 (169, 185, 209, 225, 257, 273) sts

Shaping Rnds 2 and 3: knit.

Rep Shaping Rnds 1-3 another 2 times. 153 (161, 177, 201, 217, 249, 265) sts

Work even for 10 (12, 12, 14, 14, 16, 18) rnds.

Shaping Rnd 1 (inc): *k1, m1, k to 1 st from marker, m1, k1, sm;

rep from * once more. 157 (165, 181, 205, 221, 253, 269) sts

Shaping Rnds 2 and 3: knit.

Rep Shaping Rnds 1-3 another 2 times. 165 (173, 189, 213, 229, 261, 277) sts

Begin slip-stitch pattern:

Rnd 1: using col B, k1, *sl1 wyif, k1; rep from * to end.

Rnd 2: using col B, knit.

Rnd 3: using col A, k2, *sl1 wyif, k1; rep from * to last st, k1.

Rnds 4, 5 and 6: using col A, knit.

Rnd 7: using col B, k1, *sl1 wyif, k1; rep from * to end.

Rnd 8, 9 and 10: using col B, knit.

Rnd 11: using col A, k1, *sl1 wyif, k1; rep from * to end.

Rnd 12: using col A, knit.

Rnd 13: using col B, k2, *sl1 wyif, k1; rep from * to last st, k1.

Rnds 14, 15 and 16: using col B, knit.

Rnd 17: using col A, k1, *sl1 wyif, k1; rep from * to end.

Rnd 18, 19 and 20: using col A, knit.

Work slip-stitch Rnds 1-8 once more.

Break col A, leaving tail long

enough to weave in later,
and continue in col B.

Next Rnd: knit.

Next Rnd (dec): k to side
marker, k39 (41, 45, 51, 55, 62,
66), k2tog, k to end. 164 (172,
188, 212, 228, 260, 276) sts

Work even for another 0
(0, 2, 2, 4, 4, 6) rnds.

Change to smaller needles:

Rib Rnd: *k2, p2; rep from * to end.

Work Rib Rnd another 14
times. Cast off in patt.

Sleeves (knit 2)

Using col A and larger needles, cast
on 2 (2, 2, 2, 2, 3, 3) sts, pick up and
k60 (60, 66, 74, 78, 92, 100) sts from
those held on waste yarn, cast on 2
(2, 2, 2, 2, 3, 3) sts, pm to mark beg of
rnd. 64 (64, 70, 78, 82, 98, 106) sts

Work even for 3 rnds.

Next Rnd (dec): k1, k2tog, k to
3 sts before marker, ssk, k1, sm.
62 (62, 68, 76, 80, 96, 104) sts

Rep this decrease rnd every 10th
(10th, 8th, 8th, 6th, 6th, 8th)
rnd, 8 (8, 11, 3, 13, 3, 7) times.
46 (46, 46, 70, 54, 90, 90) sts

Then rep this decrease rnd every
4th (4th, 4th, 6th, 4th, 4th, 2nd)
rnd, 3 (3, 1, 11, 3, 17, 15) times. 40
(40, 44, 48, 48, 56, 60) sts.

Work slip-stitch pattern:

Rnd 1: using col B, k1, *sl1 wyif, k1;
rep from * to 1 st from end, k1.

Break col A, leaving tail long
enough to weave in later,
and continue in col B.

Work even for 2 rnds.

Change to smaller needles.

Rib Rnd: *k2, p2; rep from * to end.

Rep Rib Rnd another 8
times. Cast off in patt.

Finishing

Weave in ends, sew up gap
at underarms, and block to
dimensions given in schematic.

3.2
PRINTED

WOODCUT

A carved block of wood from which prints are made.

Have you practis'd so long to learn to read?

WALT WHITMAN
Song of Myself

Making a hap shawl that paid homage to woodcuts was a straightforward idea. Consider the following:

1. Woodcuts were expensive to produce, so they were frequently used several times within the same book in different contexts.

Lace functions on the basis of repeats. You can repeat the same motif in different contexts and in different combinations. A pattern is formed on the basis of repeats.

2. Woodcuts were often assembled from several parts and made up of small blocks.

A hap shawl is made up of smaller parts and assembled in steps. First you work the centre triangle with yarn-overs made at the beginning of each row. Then, you pick up stitches from the yarnover loops along the edges of your triangle and work a mid-section outwards from the centre. Finally, the hap is finished with an edge that is worked perpendicular.

3. Woodcuts were cut along the wood grain.

Hap shawls are typically worked in garter stitch, which lends a nice 'grain' to the shawl and lets you see the construction.

But let us go back to a conversation I had with the Shetland lace designer Donna Smith some years ago. I was teaching a class on Faroese shawl knitting and we were comparing traditional Faroese lace charts with contemporary lace charts. Traditional Faroese charts tend not to include decreases, but only show the placement of the decorative yarnovers. Donna and I discussed how this form of lace chart felt like a visual representation of an oral tradition— an oral tradition which was very much how Donna had been taught her lace patterns. Meanwhile, I began obsessing over how we first began to think about visually representing our knowledge? When did we move from 'knit three stitches, then make your

lace stitches, then knit three...' to k3, yo, k2tog, k3 to a lace chart representing this? Was this the way that we moved at all? Maybe we started by looking at a piece of knitted lace and then started making drawings and then began telling stories? Does this matter?

So, let us look closer at how images and words work—particularly when they collide in textiles. I have often been frustrated by book historians who claim that printing gave way to 'an image culture' and 'an abundance of visual aids' as I think this ignores the visual qualities of text and lettering. Bear with me. This relates to how we also read and understand our knitting.

Woodcuts were images that allowed for rapid reproduction and uniformity; they were easy to insert into a frame already prepared with movable type and instructive books on alchemy, anatomy, astrology, astronomy and other topics used woodcuts to great effect. I have studied sixteenth-century embroidery manuals written in German and Italian with very clear charts that would be easy to work from even today; well-ordered knowledge clearly laid out in books that were disseminated across an increasingly literate world. You did not even need to understand *Frühneuhochdeutsch* (Early New High German) or Renaissance Italian to follow the instructions.

These days we have Japanese knitting books with charts so clear and concise you do not need to understand Japanese to read them. Personally I enjoy designing lace charts. Lace is essentially just a series of strategically placed holes matched by decreases. When you design a lace chart, you are working out a visual representation of a fabric for other people to follow. You sit down to work out repeats and whether your yarnovers match your decreases. I find it quite straightforward and relaxing to work out where repeats occur and where to move stitch patterns if I want specific fabric movements to occur. Yet I regularly get pattern queries from knitters who do not quite feel the same way about lace charts and who struggle to get the right result.

In the Western world, the reading eye generally moves from left to right, then we have a line break that tells the reading eye that we must move down and start from the left again. And so

we read the next line left to right. And the next one. And the next one.

If you are new to charts, you may not realise that you have to read knitting charts differently. You will transfer your usual way of reading a text to how you read a knitting chart—but a direct transfer will most likely result in trouble as repeats will not line up correctly and those strategically-placed holes and decreases will veer off into the unknown.

When we work from a knitting chart, we start at the bottom right-hand corner, and move one step to the left, then another and another, until we reach the left-hand corner. If the chart is worked flat (as with the Woodcut charts), we then move up to the next row, and begin working from the left-hand side towards the right, one tiny square at a time. When we reach the right-hand side, we move up to the next row, and begin the process all over again.

And the reason why charts are not to be read like a piece of text?

We read knitting charts in a snake-like manner because of the way we work the stitches. When we work a stitch, we move it from the left needle to the right needle. And so the reading eye needs to imitate this movement by reading the next left-hand box on the chart. As there are no line breaks in knitting, the reading eye needs to keep moving. The turning of the work at the end of a row becomes the turning of direction in the knitting chart.

This very place is where texts, textiles and the way we read things collide. This sort of movement in a text and textile is called *bouſtrophedon*.

Bouſtrophedon is Ancient Greek for 'like an ox while ploughing'. Rather than going left-to-right as in Weſtern European languages or right-to-left as in languages such as Arabic or Hebrew, *bouſtrophedon* lines keep changing direction. Right-to-left becomes left-to-right becomes right-to-left. The farmer patiently working the field with his oxen. Part of me keeps wondering if *bouſtrophedon* is the right term or if we should have coined a phrase borrowed from textiles—the movement of a shuttle is similar as is the movement contained in knitted fabrics.

The English language abounds with phrases borrowed from textile production: we *ſpin a yarn*, we *weave a ſtory*, we *tie up loose ends*, we are *kept on tenterhooks*, we *iron out creases*, we *fabricate* truths and we *patch things up*. As I began writing this book, I knew about the etymological link between the words *text* and *textile*. Both words are derived from the Latin word *texere* ('to weave') and this link is so often unpicked by scholars who enjoy wordplay, that it is almoſt its own sub-genre.

As work progressed, my thinking about the correlation between text and textile changed. The *material* qualities of both text and textile became more important: the ſtatic world of a woodcut on a page surrounded by equally ſtatic letters; the shape of a shawl and the ſtitches contained within; the ſtructure of a lace chart and what it is trying to mimic.

There is so much movement contained within these things we consider ſtatic, text and textile alike.

I ſtill do not know how we firſt began to think about visually representing knitting but I am grateful that we have ways of sharing knowledge across languages. ☞

WOODCUT SHAWL

Materials

Blacker Yarns St Kilda Laceweight
(laceweight; 347m/380 yds
per 50g skein; 100% wool)

2 skeins

Sample shown in Stac Lee

Needles Used

4 mm/US 6, circular, 80cm/32"

Gauge

16 sts x 22 rows = 10cm x 10cm / 4"
x 4" measured over blocked g st

Accessories

5 stitch markers

Waste yarn

Sizing

One size; 156cm by 64cm / 61.5"
by 25". Please see pattern notes
for sizing modifications.

Pattern Notes

This pattern is suitable for
experienced knitters.

The shawl uses the traditional
Shetland hap shawl construction: the
centre triangle is knitted and cast off
(except for one stitch), then stitches
are picked up for the lace section.

The lace section expands by
four stitches every RS row and
features a central spine.

An applied border is worked at a
90-degree angle to the shawl body
at the end. You cast on stitches, and
work them according to the chart. As
you reach the end of the border chart,
you join the last stitch of your border
to a stitch from the shawl body.

For a larger shawl, work the g st

triangle until you have 165 sts, cast off 164 sts, pick up 80 sts, m1, pick up 81 sts, work as outlined. After Chart A you have 239 sts, after Chart B you have 299 sts. After set-up for applied border you have 308 sts. Work applied border as foll: work Set-up Rows 1 and 2 once before and after Chart C. Work Chart C 51 times.

Chart Instructions

Charts A and B: WS rows are NOT charted. See below for further instructions.

Charts A and B do not show the edge sts either side of the lace chart. Remember to begin and end every row with k2.

Charts A and B do not show the centre stitch nor the entire shawl. After you have completed one side of the shawl, k1, and work the chart again.

Charts A and B: work all WS rows as follows: knit across.

Charts A and B finish with a WS row after the last RS shown on chart.

Chart C: the last st is worked together with the first st from the shawl body.

INSTRUCTIONS

Garter Stitch Triangle

Cast on 1 st.

Row 1 (RS): yo, k1. 2 sts

Row 2 (WS): yo, k2. 3 sts

Row 3: yo, k3. 4 sts

Row 4: yo, k4. 5 sts

Row 5: yo, k5. 6 sts

Row 6: yo, k6. 7 sts

Place waste yarn through mid stitch on Row 7 to indicate RS.

Row 7: yo, k to end. 8 sts

Row 7 establishes g st pattern with 1 st increased every row.

Rep Row 7 until you have 115 sts and RS facing for next row.

Remove waste yarn marking RS.

Cast off 114 sts using stretchy cast-off as foll: k2, sl these sts back to LH needle, *k2tog, k1, sl these sts back to LH needle; rep from * until 1 st rem.

Keeping rem st on your RH needle, pick up and k56 from the LH side of the g st triangle, pm, m1 (at tip of triangle), pm, pick up and k57. 115 sts

Next Row (WS): knit.

Place st markers after the first 2

sts and before the last 2 sts. These markers indicate edge sts. You now have two sides of 2 edge sts plus 55 sts, separated by 1 centre stitch.

Lace Section

Set-up Row 1 (RS): k2, sm, yo, k to marker, yo, sm, k1, sm, yo, k to marker, yo, sm, k2. 119 sts

Set-up Row 2 (WS): k to end, slipping all markers.

Work Set-up Rows 1 and 2 once more. 123 sts

Row 1: k2, work Chart A, k1, work Chart A, k2.

Continue until Chart A is completed. 199 sts

Row 39: k2, work Chart B, k1, work Chart B, k2.

Continue until Chart B is completed. 259 sts

Row 69 (RS): k2, m1, k to central st, m1, k1, m1, k to last 2 sts, m1, k2. 263 sts

Row 70 (WS): knit.

Row 71: as Row 69. 267 sts

Row 72: k to central st, kfb, k to end. 268 sts

Row 73: knit.

Applied Border

With WS facing, and using the knitted cast-on method, cast on 17 sts. Do not turn.

Set-up Row 1 (RS): k across and work last edge st tog with 1 st from shawl body. Turn.

Set-up Row 2 (WS): knit. Turn

Work Set-up Rows 1 and 2 once more.

Work Chart C 44 times across shawl body. After working the final row, 2 shawl body sts and 17 border sts rem.

Work Set-up Rows 1 and 2 twice.

Cast off rem sts as foll: k2, *put both sts back onto LH needle, k2tog tbl, k1; rep from* until end.

Finishing

Weave in ends and block to dimensions given in schematic.

Chart A

Chart B

Chart C

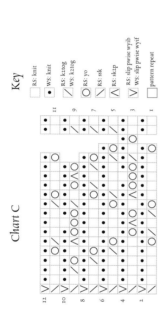

Key

RS: knit
WS: knit
RS: k2tog
WS: k2tog
RS: yo
RS: ssk
RS: sk2p
RS: slip pwise wyib
WS: slip pwise wyif
pattern repeat

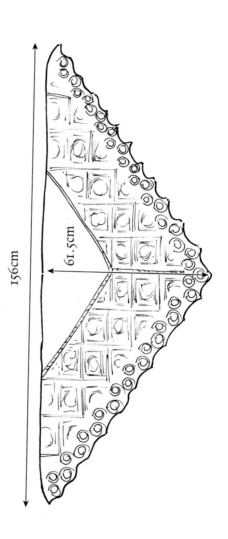

156cm

61.5cm

3·3
PRINTED

BIBLIOTHECA

Library; a collection of books.

It is good to have an end to journey towards;
but it is the journey itself that matters, in the end.

URSULA K. LE GUIN
The Left Hand of Darkness, 1969

We shot the photographs for this shawl in a library in rural Perthshire, Scotland. Innerpeffray Library, the oldest library in Scotland, was established in the 1680s by David Drummond, Lord Madertie. At first the library was housed in a small room under the eaves of the local chapel, but today the collection has grown to fill a beautiful Georgian building. I spent my day there trailing my fingers over sixteenth- and seventeenth-century books, finding treasure here and there. My favourite room was the small one beside the main reading room. I curled up in the armchair, looked out on the rolling hills dotted with sheep, and opened a book. I could have spent all day there, every day for the rest of my life.

I grew up in rural Denmark in a working-class family. They worked as farm hands, factory workers, cleaners, and kitchen assistants. We never had much money, but everybody made stuff. There was a steady supply of handmade garments, knitted jumpers and interesting paintings, and my great-grandmother taught me to knit when I was very young.

My small hometown grew up along the railway stretching west from Copenhagen. While it didn't have much going for it (although it did have an ever-struggling football team), my town did have a local library to which my grandmother took me frequently. We'd park our bikes at the back of the building, go through the back entrance door, up the stairs, hand in our returned books at the desk to the right (this is when the smell of the library would always hit me), then we'd turn right, go up another flight of stairs, up up up as quickly as my little legs would carry me, and then on the first floor (breath), I'd turn right into the children's section. The first few shelves on the left were for toddlers (eye roll), but then came my section filled with

exciting books: Lloyd Alexander, Astrid Lindgren, Diana Wynne Jones. It was always a treat and in the library nobody cared that we couldn't afford to heat the house or that my trousers were made from curtains.

As a working-class kid, my local library made me feel as though I had a right to belong in the world and to ask questions. I stood taller inside the library. And as my teenage years arrived, I began collecting words and poems like others collected romantic relationships. My friends broke hearts, I broke book spines. At home I inherited my great-great-uncle's art history books. He had subscribed to a series of hardbacks on Great World Art in the 1960s. I devoured them. Slowly I began acquiring books, longing for the day I'd have a library of my own. My room was a small fortress of library loans, craft projects and a dog pillow. Making and reading became escape routes from my small railway town and a family life that, while loving, was sometimes chaotic.

This working-class kid wound up at university and the departmental library turned out be the most important one in my life. It was a glass cage in a concrete building, but it had more books than I could ever read. I spent many, many happy hours in there, and I somehow never even made it beyond the first five aisles. Outside the glass cage, I sat on sofas drinking coffee with other word magpies with matching book fortresses. Inside the glass cage, I had a table stacked with books and a note with my name on it. I had a small claim of ownership; a table of my own.

Later, my first apartment would exhibit the interior design style of a well-visited second-hand bookshop. In my student days, I had begun collecting books, drawing up elaborate routes to the most obscure in my Copenhagen neighbourhood and visit them regularly trying to get the anglophone books before anybody else. Now my apartment was a place where time fell into the cracks between the floorboards and it had bookshelves double-stacked with promises: *read me, read me, read me.* I put French film posters up on my walls and had house plants. I had no idea who I was.

Moving from Denmark to the U.K., I gave away most of my books. It was a freeing experience, saying goodbye to a lot of bad memories. These days I share my bookshelves with another reader. They are still double-stacked but with books that are being read, not collected. I still see ghosts on my bookshelves. Outlines of all the books I gave away. All the different paths I did not take. All the promises whispered to me are now being heard by other people.

Now that I am a knitter, similar promises are made by yarn. The whispered promise of a cardigan rings as true as those coyly offered by the books. I enter a yarn shop, a bookshop or a lending library—and I imagine what my life would be like if I wore a glorious hand-knitted cardigan while reading Virginia Woolf. I can re-invent myself through making and reading...over, and over, and over.

The small girl clad in curtain-trousers reading on the floor of her small-town library has become a grown woman with a hand-dyed, handmade shawl reading in a seventeenth-century lending library.

What a strange story. ☞

BIBLIOTHECA SHAWL

Materials

Ripples Crafts Quinag Bluefaced Leicester (4ply; 400m/435 yds per 100g skein; 100% Bluefaced Leicester)

2 skeins

Sample in Copper Beech

Needles Used

4mm/US 6, circular, 80cm/32"

Gauge

17 sts x 30 rows = 10cm x 10cm / 4" x 4" measured over blocked st st

Accessories

4 stitch markers

Sizing

One size; 220cm by 74 cm/ 86.5" by 29"

Pattern Notes

This pattern is suitable for intermediate knitters.

The shawl is worked from the top down.

Section A is increased by 4 sts every RS of the shawl.

Section A is NOT charted.

Section B is increased by 2 sts every row.

Section B is charted.

Section B charts show every row of the worked piece.

Note that the shawl as written uses both skeins in their entirety. Check your gauge carefully and weigh your yarn before beginning to ensure you will have enough yarn. If you are a loose knitter, you may need additional yarn or opt to go down a needle size (eg. 3.75mm/US 5).

INSTRUCTIONS

Cast on 2 sts.

Rows 1-9: knit.

Row 10 (RS): k2, turn work 90 degrees, pick up and k 1 st from each of the 5 g st ridges along the side edge. Pick up and k 2 sts from cast-on edge. 9 sts

Row 11 (WS): k2, p5, k2.

Section A

(not charted)

Set up

Row 1 (RS; inc): k2, pm, yo, k2, m1, pm, k1, pm, m1 k2, yo, pm, k2. 13 sts

Row 2 (WS): k2, sm, p to last 2 sts slipping all markers, k2.

Pattern

Row 3 (inc): k2, sm, yo, p to marker, m1, sm, p1, sm, m1, p to marker, yo, sm, k2.

Row 4 and all WS rows: k2, sm, p to last 2 sts slipping all markers, k2.

Rows 5 and 7 (inc): k2, sm, yo, k to marker, m1, sm, k1, sm, m1, k to marker, yo, sm, k2.

Row 8: k2, sm, p to last 2 sts

slipping all markers, k2.

Rows 3-8 establish pattern with 12 sts increased per pattern repeat.

Work Rows 3-8 another 13 times. 181 sts

Work Rows 7 and 8 once. 185 sts

On the final row remove stitch markers from the middle of the shawl, but keep the ones marking the edges.

Section B

Rows 1-22: work Chart A once. 229 sts

Rows 23-44: work Chart B once. 273 sts

Rows 45-66: work Chart C once. 317 sts

Rows 67-88: work Chart D once. 361 sts

Rows 89-110: work Chart E once. 405 sts

Rows 111-132: work Chart F once. 449 sts

Rows 133-136: knit, removing all markers.

Cast off as foll: k2, *slip both sts back onto LH needle, k2tog tbl, k1; rep from * to end.

Finishing

Weave in ends and block to
dimensions given in schematic.

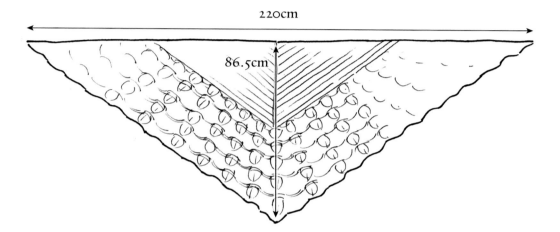

220cm

86.5cm

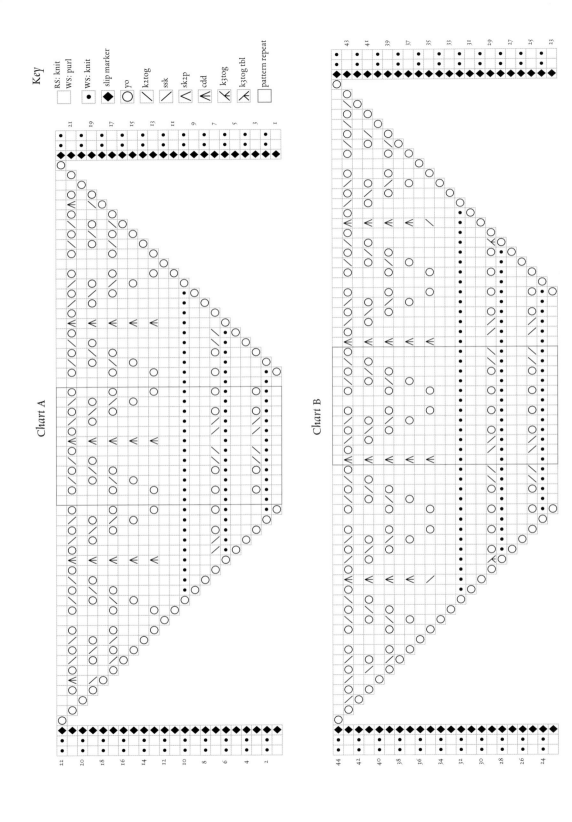

Key

| RS: knit WS: purl |
| WS: knit |
| slip marker |
| yo |
| k2tog |
| ssk |
| sk2p |
| cdd |
| k3tog |
| k3tog tbl |
| pattern repeat |

Chart A

Chart B

Chart C

Chart D

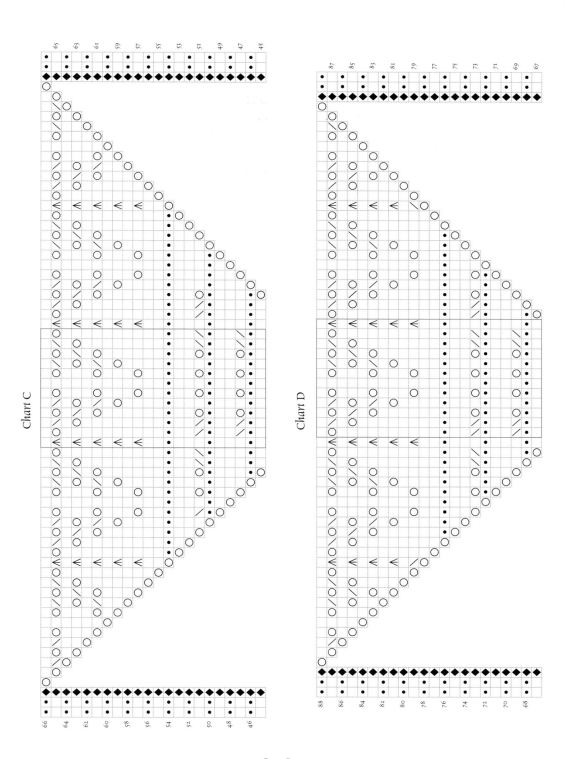

Chart E

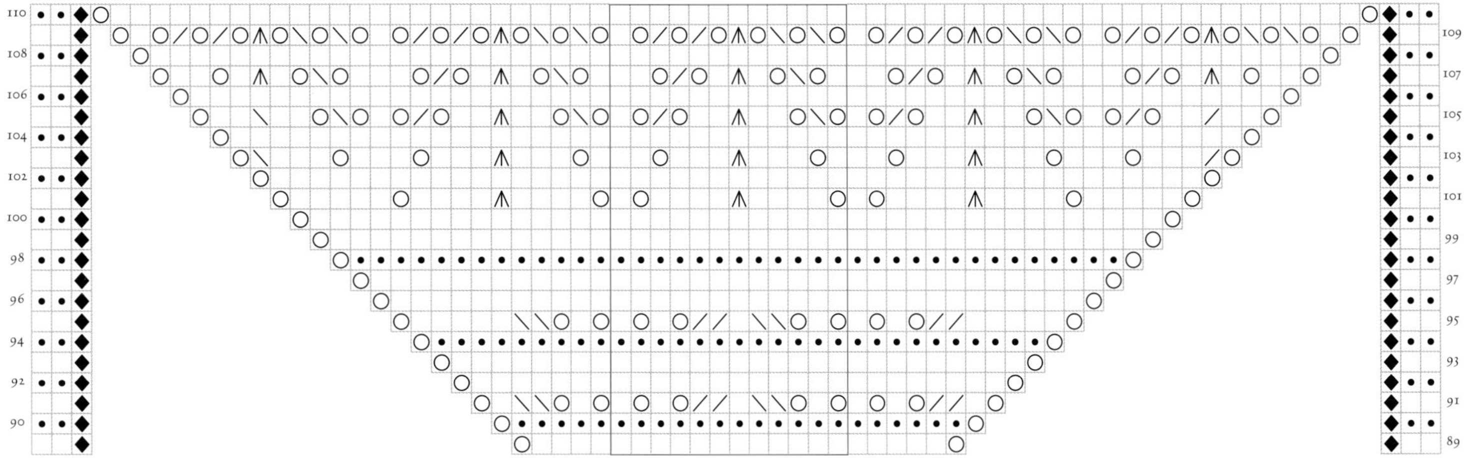

Chart F

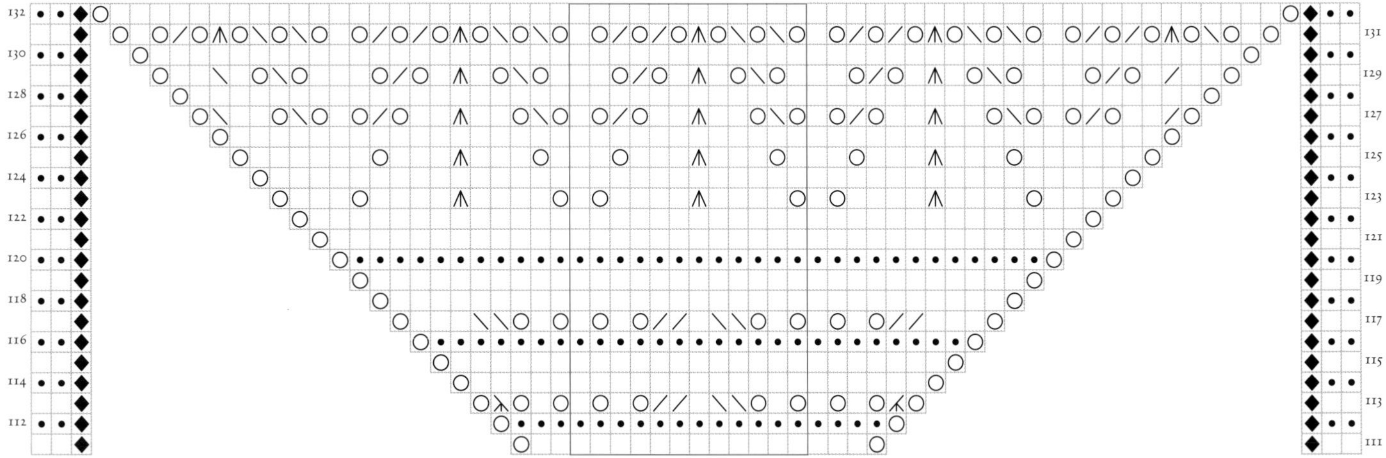

Key

RS: knit
WS: purl
WS: knit
slip marker
yo
k2tog
ssk
sk2p
cdd
k3tog
k3tog tbl
pattern repeat

ABBREVIATIONS

1/1 LT (Left Twist) skipping first st, knit the second st on LH needle through the back loop, then knit both the first and the second sts on LH needle together through the back loop, slipping both sts off LH needle

1/1 RT (Right Twist) k2tog leaving sts on LH needle, then knit first st on LH needle, then slip both sts off LH needle

beg beginning

cdd central double decrease: slip 2 sts knitwise together, knit 1, pass slipped sts over

col colour

dec decrease

DPN(s) double-pointed needle(s)

est established

foll following

GSR German short rows; see Special Techniques, page 131

g st garter stitch

inc increase

k knit

kfb knit front and back

k2tog knit two sts together

kyok [k1, yo, k1] into one st — two sts increased

kwise knitwise

LH left-hand

M metre

m1 make one (lifted increase)

p purl

patt pattern

pm place marker

prev previous

pwise purlwise

rem remaining

rep repeat

rnd(s) round(s)

RH right-hand

RS right side

sk2p slip 1, knit two together, pass slipped st over

skyk slip 3rd st on LH needle over first 2 sts and off needle; k1, yo, k1

sl slip (pwise unless noted)

sm slip marker

ssk slip one kwise, slip one pwise, knit two slipped sts together

st(s) stitch(es)

st st stocking st

tog together

w&t wrap and turn; see Special Techniques, page 131

WS wrong side

wyib with yarn in back

wyif with yarn in front

yo yarnover

SPECIAL TECHNIQUES

All techniques shown are also available on my website: kariebookish.net under Tutorials. You can find illustrative photos there as well as more in-depth commentary.

Steeking cutting your knitting (as used in Vellum, page 9)

First, some reassurance. Knitting unravels downwards and not sidewards, so don't worry about your hard work falling to pieces. However, it is important that you secure your sts well before cutting. This tutorial uses the crochet slip stitch method which my grandmother taught me.

1. Identify the steek sts. Vellum has 6 sts, but other projects may have other numbers. With Vellum the first (1, 2 and 3) and last 3 sts (4, 5, and 6) of the rnd make up the steek sts with the beg of the rnd falling between sts 3 and 4.

2. Weave in all loose ends away from the steek sts.

3. Using high-contrast sewing thread, baste a line from top to bottom of cardigan between steek sts 3 and 4. Use this basting line to identify your surrounding sts.

4. Using contrast yarn of a similar weight, begin to work crochet slip stitches on top of steek stitch 2.

5. Make a slipknot on your hook.

6. Push the hook through the cast-on edge of work through the centre of steek stitch 2, catch yarn at back, and draw a loop through the fabric and the slipknot. 1 loop on hook

7. Insert your hook into the first V of the vertical line of the steek stitches stacked on top of each other, catch yarn at back, and draw a loop through the fabric and the loop on your hook. 1 loop on hook

8. Continue to work your way to the top of the garment, taking care to only work steek stitch 2 throughout, and not to catch another parts of the garment.

9. At the top of the garment, finish by working a slip stitch across the cast-off edge. Cut yarn and pull through rem loop on hook.

10. Following steps 4-9, work a similar vertical line of crochet slip stitches on top of steek st 5.

11. After you have secured the stitches, prepare to cut between steek sts 3 and 4 (where your basting thread runs). Use sharp scissors to cut the small horizontal lines/ladders between the sts. Take care not to cut anything else.

12. Pick up sts using the ladders between the body of your garment and steek sts 1 or 6. You may cover the raw steek edges with a ribbon for added security and/or aesthetic reasons.

One-Row Buttonhole (as used in Vellum, page 13)

1. Sl 1 st pwise wyif.

2. Move working yarn to back and leave until step 5.

3. *sl 1 st pwise, pass prev st over; rep from * until 3 sts have been cast off.

4. Place last cast off st on RH needle back on LH needle. Turn work.

5. Move working yarn to back.

6. Using the cable method, cast on 4 sts.

7. Move yarn to front. Turn work.

8. Sl 1 st kwise and pass extra cast-on st over it.

Three-needle cast-off (as used in Incunabula, page 34)

1. Hold two needles so the RS are on the inside, facing each other, and you have the same amount of sts on both needles.

2. Using a third needle, knit one stitch from the front needle together with one stitch from the back needle.

3. Repeat step 2, so you have two sts on the RH needle.

4. Pass first stitch over the second as in a normal cast-off.

5. Repeat steps 2-4 until all sts have been cast off.

w&t wrap and turn short rows (as used in Incunabula, page 56)

1. Slip next st on to RH needle, moving the working yarn to the opposite side of work between needles.

2. Slip st back to LH needle.

3. Turn work ready to work in opposite direction.

4. Work wrap tog with wrapped st when working across st.

GSR German short rows (as used in Marginalia, page 99)

GSR Right Side:

1. With WS facing, slip st purlwise from LH needle to RH needle wyif.

2. Pull the yarn OVER the RH needle to the back of the work (RS). This will make the slipped st look distorted

or doubled—as though it were actually two sts rather than one.

3. Bring yarn forward between the two needles.

4. Begin purling, making sure the tension is a bit tighter for the first four sts. Work as specified in patt.

GSR Wrong Side:

1. With RS facing, bring yarn forward between the two needles.

2. Slip st purlwise from LH needles to RH needle wyif.

3. Pull the yarn OVER the RH needle to the back of the work (WS). This will make the slipped st look distorted or doubled — as though it were actually two sts rather than one.

4. Begin knitting, making sure the tension is a bit tighter for the first four sts. Work as specified in patt.

Picking up GSR double sts

1. Work to the distorted/ doubled stitch.

2. Work this st as a k2tog.

ACKNOWLEDGEMENTS

This Thing of Paper would not exist without the support and generosity of seven hundred and twenty-five Kickstarter backers. Thank you so much for believing in this book: you have been such great cheerleaders throughout. I owe you so much gratitude.

The backers A, Adele Geras, Adrienne, Adrienne Williams, Agoetz2, Ainsley, Alessandra Parsons, Alex Broadbent, Alex Tinsley, Alexis, Alice, Alice Dawson, Alice Elsworth, Alice Owen, Alison, Alison Beadnell, Alison Gilhooly, Alison Keys, Alison Mayne, Alison Powell, Alison Semeonoff, Alix Pearson, Allison Thistlewood, Amanda Cooke, Amanda Laing, Amanda Luebke, Amber Weinberg, Amelia Hodsdon, Ami Martinez Rowland, Amie Falch, Amy Bednarz, Amy Doran, Amy Palmer, Amy Wolff, Andrea, Andrea Harman, Andrea Napier, Andrea Richardson, Ange Sewell, Angela Dent, Angela Mehlert, Anggerek, Anj Medhurst, Anjeanette Milner, Anna, Anna Cosar, Anna Elliott, Anna Feldman, Anna Fisk, Anna McNally, Annastasia Gallaher, Anne, Anne, Anne Anthony, Anne Howe, Anne Kuell, Anne Murphy, Anne Murray, Anne Sowell, Anne Thrall-Nash, Anne-Marie Scott, Annemarie Schuetz, Annemarie Van Putten, Annette LaCivita, Anni Howard, Annie Wilson, Annika Barranti Klein, Anthea Willis, Arla Kean, Aya Tanaka, Backpackmidwife, Barb French, Barbara Bonn, Barbara Ellis, Barbara Stern, Bastian Müller, Bekky Bush, Beth Peat, Beth Raymond, Beth Wallace, Bethan Jenkins, Betsy Ioannou, Bristol, Bron Livingstone, C Rand, C Thomson, Caitlin Saraphis, Caitlin Bradley, Carina Spencer, Carol Christie, Carol Feller, Carol Fieldhouse, Carol Kepshire, Carol Rhoades, Carol Seitz, Carol Sue Desrochers, Carol Williams, Carole Davies Hooper, Carole Reboul, Carole Satchwell, Caroline Lloyd, Caroline Stead, Caroline Wright, Carolyn, Carolyn Sue Jenkins, Cassandra Leszczynski, Cat Yee, Cate Fitt, Catherine, Catherine Cornwell, Catherine Shaw, Catherine

Sykes, Cathy Cooper, Cathy Davies, Cathy Scott, Cathy Silver, Cecilia Hewett, Celia Edwards, Celia Maughan, Charlene Anderson, Charlotte Brett, Charlotte Claridge, Charlotte Topsfield, Cheryl Alcorn, Cheryl Collins, Cheryl Hedlund, Cheryl Koester,

Cheryl McLeod, Cheryl Vowcicefski, Chris Bath, Christie, Christina Cunningham, Christina Estrup, Christina Kingsmill, Christina White, Christine Grabowski, Christine Harding, Christine Worrall, Ciara Roughneen, Claire, Claire Leach, Claire Williams, Clara Parkes, Clare Woods, Courtenay Nicol, Craftyamoeba, Crystal DeGrote Heppe, Daisy Schrock, Dala Beld, Dave Bennett, David, David Curran, David Tavakoli, Dawn Hummerstone, Dbexx, Deb, Deb Braak, Deb Bramham, Debora Bradley, Deborah Barr, Deborah Magness, Deborah Robson, Debra Muir, Debra Riley, Delores Whiteman, Desiree Goodall, Destiny Itano, Diane, Diane Bobal, Diane Collinson, Dianna, Dianna Repp, Dianne Blackett, Dieuwke van Mulligen, Ditte Bentzen, Donna, Dorean Davis, Doreen Hamilton, Dorian Stiefel, Dyan, Dylan Crawford, E M Dunbar, Edith Michler, Eeh, Eileen Brown, Elaine Anderson, Elaine Froneberger, Elaine

Weston, Eleanor Chalkley, Eleonora Knowland, Eleyne, Elin Lund, Eline, Elisa, Elise Watson, Elizabeth, Elizabeth, Elizabeth Bridges White, Elizabeth Harvey, Elizabeth Lewis, Elizabeth Martin, Elizabeth Wynn, Ella Smith, Ellen Berman, Ellen Forsyth, Elouise Kevern, Emanuelle, Emily Dibdin, Emily Lind, Emily Owen, Emma, Emma Dautlon, Emma Heasman-Hunt, Emma Knowles, Emma Wynn, Ercil Howard-Wroth, Erika Heald, Erin Sostock, Esther Bozak, Eva Fornazaric, Eve Hoffenkamp, Eveline Groot, Ewan Spence, Fay Clark, Fiona, Fiona Collins, Fiona Cooper, Fiona Hackland, Fiona Hunter, Fiona Macdonald, Fleur Parker, Francesca Brettell, Francesca Macchi, Françoise Peppiatt, Franziska, Freyalyn Close, Frida Haro, Gabi, Gail Donaldson, Genevieve O'Shea, Gillian Harkness, Gillian Matthews, Gina Flansbury, Gina Ritchie, Ginevra M, Ginny MacDonald, Gwen Casey, Hailey, Hannah Greene, Hanne Lehmann-Taylor, Harriet Kennedy, Hazel D'Aguiar, Heather Kiernan, Heather McCloud-Huff, Heather Peterson, Helen Courtney, Helen Dayananda, Helen Gilman, Helen McCorry, Helen Mears, Helen Rice, Helen Wherrett, Helena Bruce, Helena Thomas, HelenMc, Hester

Lean, Holly, Isabel Jordan, Isabelle Burnet, Isla, Isobel Cutforth, Jackie, Jackie Palmer, Jacqueline Manni, James Edwards, James LaMee, James Neilson, Jamie Miller, Jan Martin, Jane Ball, Jane Carroll, Jane Cooper, Jane DelFavero, Jane Hickman, Jane Hull, Jane Lithgow, Jane M Kieffer Rath, Jane Travers, Jane Wheeler, Jane White, Janet Barracough, Janice Taylor, Jannika Hammarbrink, Jean Andress, Jean Ashley, Jean Yeomans, Jeannine, Jen Coican Hovis, Jen Stilwell, Jena Burges, Jeni Reid, Jenni, Jennifer, Jennifer Aves, Jennifer Mohr, Jennifer Smith, Jenny, Jenny Grimes, Jenny Irvine, Jenny Moran, Jenny Richens, Jenny Simpson, Jeny MacPhee, Jesper Lillesoe, Jessica Martin, Jessie McKitrick, Jill Shepherd, Jillian Edwards, Jinny Jerome, Jo Cross, Jo Kelly, Joan Duhamel, Joanne Burroughs, Jocelyn Shaw, Jody Pruett, Joeli Kelly, Johanna Zetterqvist, Johanne Jasmin, Jordan Wright, Josh Moll, Joyce Neema, Judi Anderson Seal, Judit Sogan, Judith Draper, Judith Hunter, Judith Korving, Judy Noah, Julia Benson-Slaughter, Julia Duffield, Julia Schlingelhoff, Julia Walton, Julie Abbott, Julie Carpenter, Julie Elliott, Julie Nelson Rhodes, Julie Stauffer, Julie Walker, Justine Lopez, Kairi, Karen, Karen, Karen Borovszky, Karen Clyde, Karen Gerstner, Karen Howlett, Karen Lafferty, Karen Mardahl, Karen Pior, Karen Preston, Karen Rodger, Karen Skriver Lauger, Karen Styles, Karyn Cook, Kat Anderberg, Kate, Kate Atherley, Kate Bostwick, Kate Davies, Kate Gregory, Kate Heppell, Kate McCarthy-Gilmore, Kate Woolley, Katharine Creighton-Griffiths, Katharine Patterson, Katherine Dunhill, Katherine Hegarty, Katherine Mackinnon, Katherine Nagl, Katheryn Haverinen, Kathleen Hinchliffe, Kathleen Meggitt, Kathreen Kruse, Kathryn Easterford, Kathy Harry, Katie, Katie Bricker, Katie Ingram, Katie McGettigan, Katie Pearce, Kay Bingham, Kay Muir, Kelli, Kelly Arbuckle, KG Baker, Kim, Kim M, Kimberly Park, Kirsten Marie Øveraas, KM Bedigan, Kris Montague, Kristan MacIntyre, Krystal A Lowe, L Gerrard, Laila Jensen, Larissa Barrie, Lars Rains, Laura Allport, Laura Fazzio, Laura Jones, Laura Reid, Laurel Faye, Lauren, Lauren Rodriguez, Lauren Smith, Laurie DuBois, Lee Meredith, Leigh Dunlap, Leith Macdonald, Lene Rothe, Leona-Jayne Kelly, Lesley Kramer, Lesley Robinson, Lesley Taylor, Libby Henshelwood, Libby Newhouse, Lin James, Linda Ballinger, Linda Buckert,

Linda Gregory, Linda Henderson, Linda Mitchell, Linda Randall, Lindsay Roberts, Lindy Taylour, Lisa Jayne Canham, Lisa Morota, Lisa Risager, Lisbeth Klastrup, Lissa Lee, Liz, Liz Marley, Liz Pilfold, Lori LaFrance, Lori Schmieder Burton, Lorna Reid, Louisa Stratton, Louise, Louise, Louise Kelman, Louise Pritchard, Louise Reilly, Louise Scollay, Louise Sylva, Lucia Jackson, Lucy, Lucy Burns, Lucy Lyons Willis, Lucy Sloan, Lucy Tennison, Lyle Hale, Lyndsey Blackwood, Lynne, Lynne M. Thomas, Lynne Moore, Lynne Rowe, M Scott, Maddie Harvey, Madeleine Shepherd, Madeleine van Adrighem, Maggie Rapach, Mai Lee, Mairead Hardy, Mandy Sturman, Manja Vogelsang, Marc Reynolds, Margaret Chess, Margaret Tout, Maria MacInnes, Marie Irshad, Mariel Plancarte-Meade, Marilyn Nance, Marina Moskowitz, Marion Enns, Mark Davis, Martha, Martinus, Mary Alderton, Mary Connerty, Mary Gordon, Mary Graham, Mary Humphrey, Mary Jackson, Mary L Henze, Mary Wright, Mary-Helen Ward, Mary!, Maureen Heddle, May Bishop, May Linn Bang, Maylin, Maylin Scott, Meg Roper, Megan Lyerla, Meghan Jones, Mei Cheung, Melinda Bilecki, Melissa, Mette, Michele Bernstein, Michele Galloway, Michele Mudd,

Michele Pallmer, Michelle Gregory, Michelle Hazell, Michelle Lincoln, Mindy Wilkes, Miren, Monica Gill, Morag Gray, Morgen S Daily, Myriam Stricker, Nadine Haarich, Nancy, Nancy Coope, Nancy Nordquist, Nancy Ryan, Nancy Shelley, Nancy Wright, Natalia Uribe Wilson, Natalie Legg, Natalie Servant, Natalie Shipton, Natalya Pica Del Canto, Nathalie Ruebsteck, Nia Kirwin, Nic Rudd, Nicola Blay, Nicola Brand, Nicola Rutterford, Nobutterfly, Nora Howley, Orlane Bienfait-Luna, Pamela, Pamela Syme, Pamela Wynne Butler, Paola Guardini, Pat Blain, Patricia Shaw, Paula McKeown, Peggy Laipple, Penny Jenkins, Peppermint, Pernille Friis, Peter Clay, Philip Thompson, Philippa Vennall, Philippina Wijtmans, Pobblea, Rachael, Rachael Clayson-Robertson, Rachael Prest, Rachel Ali, Rachel Anderson, Rachel Brown, Rachel Carmichael, Rachel McSweeney, Rachelle Maddison, Rebecca Jones, Rebecca Prentice, Rebekka Kinimond Carlson, Rhiannon Don, Rhiannon Reid, Rhiannon Sivewright, Risa Royer, Rita Taylor, Ros Aitken, Ros Martin, Rosamund Rodriguez, Rosemary Fartch, Rosemary Moore, Rosemary Murphy, Rosie McCarthy, Ruth, Ruth Klema, Ruth Vorstman, S White, Sadie

Slater, Sally Amanda Sonnex, Sally Carter, Sam Bytheway Carr, Samantha Holland, Sandra Cox, Sandra Fleming, Sandy Hall, Sara Foster, Sara Lamb, Sara Leith, Sara Welham, Sarah, Sarah, Sarah Baker, Sarah Campbell, Sarah Clarkson, Sarah Ford, Sarah Hume, Sarah Jane Humke, Sarah Jones, Sarah Learmonth, Sarah Lewis, SarahLouise MacAdie, Sean Davern, Senta Niederegger, Seraphima Cyranek, Severine Grelois, Shanna Hollich, Shannon Hobbs, Shannon Okey, Shannon Robalino, Shanthi P, Shari, Shari Hemsley, Sharon Auerbach-Sim, Sharon Weiss, Shauna Reeves, Shawn Van Dusen, Sheila Hewitt, Sheryl S. Allred, Shirley Renicker, Shirley Suzuki, Shobha Kazinka, Shuna Marr, Signe Strømgaard, Sigrun Möller, Simon Harris, SL Mills, Sofie, Sonya Philip, Stacie, Steffi, Steph, Steph Taylor, Stephanie, Stephanie Burns, Stephanie Wischhusen, Sue Blacker, Sue Evance, Susan Anthony, Susan Crawford, Susan Hammond Jones, Susan Hanlon, Susan Hobkirk, Susan Housley, Susan Jackson, Susan Quillan, Susan Simonton, Susan Wheel, Susannah, Susanne Wiesen, Suzanne Elizabeth, Suzanne Moses, Suzie Blackman, Svm!, Sylvia MacKay, Sylvia McNally, Sylvie, T, T M Bird, Tania Ashton Jones, Teagan Longfellow, Teal Gamgee, Ted Woodward-Partridge, Teresa Baldwin, Terry W, The Bluemont Dunning family, Therese Wallstedt, Thien-Kieu Lam, Tina M. Moser, Tine Jensen, Tine L, Tinne, Toni-anne Alyn, Tori Seierstad, Tracey, Tracy Holroyd-Smith, Tricia Lundie, Ulrika Fröberg, Una Morrison, Valerie Newton, Valerie Oliner, Vanessa Cameron, Vicki Adams, Vicki Martin, Vicky Barrett, Victoria Appel Delard, Victoria Bennett, Victoria Davies, Victoria Hadlow, Victoria Phillips, Victoria Selnes, Vivienne Gray, Vivienne Seal, Vivienne Upton, Vonnie McDermott, Wei-Lin Allen, Wendy Baird, Wendy Baldwin, Wendy Morris, Wendy Peterson, Woolly Wormhead, Y N, Yumi Shimada, Yvette Campbell, Yvonne Davies, Ziggie Nybo Andersen, Zoe Armstrong, Zoe Jean.

Thank you to family and friends. Kathleen and the rest of the Frasers. Tina, Torben and Inge. I nearly lost some of you. I am so glad you are still with us. Christina, Ellie, Paula, Kirsten, Ziggie, Oliver, Hattie, Lauren, Ben and Anna for keeping me on a relatively even keel in choppy seas.

Thank you to the book team. Amelia for the numerous Beastie Boys references in her tech editing notes. Kate G. for patiently looking up all the weird words which I subsequently removed. Signe for the long, meandering Skype chats. Jules Akel for the design knowledge and good humour. Michelle for lending a third pair of eyes when needed. Elly, Katherine, and Liz for helping me out with sample knitting. Julie Nelson Rhodes for giving me a solid visual framework.

Thank you to the yarn supporters. Sonja of Blacker Yarns for her unwavering passion and belief. Larissa of Travelknitter for the perfect red yarn and solid dead-pan humour. Sheila of DyeNinja for her enthusiasm and belief in the healing properties of home-baked scones. Helen of Ripples Crafts for continual support and advice (and steady supply of dog photos).

Thank you to all the people who advised and shaped This Thing of Paper. Lara Heggarty at Innerpeffray Library for her kindness, hospitality, knowledge, and expert tea-making. The staff at the Gutenberg Museum, Mainz (especially Martina Illner) who let me work in the most amazing environment. The test knitters who gave their time and expertise — you went beyond the call of duty. Susan, Woolly, Kat, Bristol, Katya, Louise, Felix, Tom, Meg, Michelle, Naomi, Alison, Allison, Rachel, Jo, LJ, Nora, Kate A., Isla and Kate H. for all the wise words — yet again proving that knitting is solidarity and community. Charles Lock and Bruce Clunies-Ross for indulging me all those years ago. Kath for the lift to the train. Marina, Lynn, and Linda for their generosity of spirit and support.

Thank you to the pen pal I had as a child who wrote me beautifully calligraphed letters. I can no longer remember your name, but you made me think about the materiality of writing at a very young age.

Thank you to every librarian who befriends a child.

Thank you to David, as always, for everything. This book would not exist without you.

And, finally, thank you to my beautiful great-grandmother Lilly, who taught me to knit when I was four.

This book is dedicated to Alan Fraser who sadly never saw it finished. ✳

SELECTED BIBLIOGRAPHY

BENJAMIN, WALTER: *Illuminations* (ed. H. Arendt; H. Zohn, transl.), Fontana Press, London, 1973 (1992)

BOLTER, JAY DAVID: *Writing Space: Computers, Hypertext, and the Remediation of Print*, Lawrence Erlbaum Associates, Mahwah, New Jersey, 2001

CAVALLO, G. AND CHARTIER, R.: *A History of Reading in the West*, (L. G. Cochrane, trans.), Polity Press, Cambridge, 1999

ELIOT, SIMON AND ROSE, JONATHAN (eds.): *A Companion to the History of the Book*, Wiley-Blackwell, Chichester, 2009

FEBVRE, LUCIEN AND MARTIN, HENRI-JEAN: *The Coming of the Book*, Verso, London, 1976 (1990)

FINKLESTEIN, D. AND MCCLEERY, A.: *An Introduction to Book History*, Routledge, Abingdon, 2012

GENETTE, GERARD: *Paratexts — Thresholds of Interpretation* (J. E. Lewin, trans.), Cambridge University Press, Cambridge, 1997

JOHNS, ADRIAN: *The Nature of the Book — Print and Knowledge in the Making*, The University of Chicago Press, Chicago, 1998

MANGUEL, ALBERTO: *A History of Reading*, Flamingo, London, 1997

MCGANN, JEROME: *The Textual Condition*, Princeton University Press, Princeton, 1991

MEGGS, PHILLIP B.: *A History of Graphic Design*, John Wiley & Sons, Ltd, New York, 1983 (Third edition, 1998)

ONG, WALTER: *Orality and Literacy — The Technologizing of the Word*, Routledge, London, 1982 (2002)

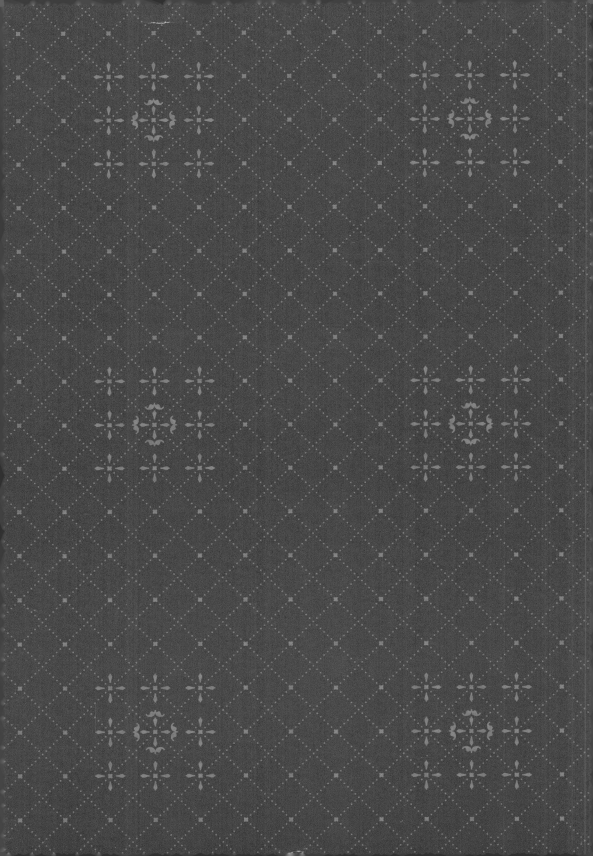